D0667143

OBAMA'S
AMERICA

For Vibeke, Nadja, Martin and Lea

OBAMA'S AMERICA

Carl Pedersen

EDINBURGH UNIVERSITY PRESS

973.932
0B 15p

Edinburgh University Press Ltd
22 George Square, Edinburgh
www.euppublishing.com

Typeset in Palatino by
Servis Filmsetting Ltd, Stockport, Cheshire, and
printed and bound in Great Britain by
CPI Antony Rowe, Chippenham and Eastbourne

A CIP record for this book is available from the
British Library

ISBN 978 0 7486 3894 9 (hardback)

Contents

Great men make history, but only such history as it is possible for them to make. Their freedom of achievement is limited by the necessities of their environment.

C. L. R. James, *The Black Jacobins* (1938)

History does not refer merely, or even principally, to the past. On the contrary, the great force of history comes from the fact that we carry it within us, are unconsciously controlled by it in many ways, and history is literally *present* in all that we do.

James Baldwin, 'Unnameable Objects, Unspeakable Crimes' (1965)

Introduction

This book is an exercise in what Theodore Draper called 'present history'. Draper believed that it was possible to provide a certain depth of understanding of contemporary events if they were put into historical perspective even without the benefit of the distance of time. He regarded the present as 'evanescent' and wrote for the reader interested in seeing the stream of current events in a larger context.[1]

The election of 2008 seemed as if it were made for the kind of history that Draper advocated. Barack Obama won the Democratic nomination and the general election in part because of his message of change, a break with the recent past. Yet his writings and speeches were replete with a sense of history, a conscious attempt to do for American politics what Draper had sought to do for the writing of history – offer more than ephemeral soundbites by reminding voters of the progress achieved in the past as a guide for the direction the United States could take in the future.

Reflecting on the twentieth century at the cusp of the twenty-first, the philosopher Richard Rorty distinguished between what he called agents and spectators. Spectators regarded the US as an irredeemably unjust society. They were content to cultivate a pose of undetached disgust with the US and therefore believed that any action undertaken to change the current state of affairs was futile. Agents, on the other hand, were not averse from critique of the American national character, but sought to improve American society by fighting against injustice.

In looking back to the dawn of the twentieth century, however, Rorty saw hope for the twenty-first century. He emphasized that 'our national character is still in the making' and offered a prediction for the future by drawing on the past.

> Few in 1897 would have predicted the Progressive Movement, the forty-hour week, Women's Suffrage, the New Deal, the Civil Rights Movement, the successes of second-wave feminism, or the Gay Rights Movement. Nobody in 1997 can know that America will not, in the course of the next century, witness even greater moral progress.[2]

Obama also represented the 'national character still in the making.' The first African American president was the product of a mixed marriage and grew up in the only US state that had always had a majority–minority population and in the world's largest Muslim nation.

The year 2008 will certainly be remembered as the year when the US elected its first African American president. It also offered a number of history lessons that will surely form a substantial part of subsequent studies of the election and its aftermath. This book is an attempt to engage with these history lessons. The first Part, Obama's America, tells the story of demographic changes that will likely change the nature of American national identity. It examines the role of grassroots organizations that contributed to the kind of agency that Rorty spoke of and how they may influence the way Obama will govern the nation.

The second Part, Obama's World, attempts to map out the contours of an Obama Doctrine in foreign policy by looking at how his identity shaped his views on the US role in the world and how he, in turn, has been influenced by his foreign policy advisers. It examines the challenges Obama faces in confronting a post-American world in which the US is no longer the sole superpower.

At time of writing, it is less than five years since Obama burst onto the national stage with his speech at the 2004

Introduction

Democratic Convention. During that short time, he became only the third African American senator since Reconstruction, he beat a formidable adversary, Hillary Rodham Clinton, for the Democratic presidential nomination, and he won a substantial victory in the general election against his Republican rival, John McCain. It is too soon to tell whether Obama will prove the transformative president that so many hope he will be. Inspired by the example of Martin Luther King, Jr, Obama often declared on the campaign trail that 'the arc of history is long, but it bends towards justice'. Hopefully, this modest book will provide some tentative answers as to whether Barack Obama will succeed in bending the arc of history.

A number of colleagues were kind enough to take the time to read parts of the book and offer sage comments and incisive criticisms. I would like to thank Edward Ashbee, Niels Bjerre-Poulsen, Ray Haberski and Per Knudsen for their help along the way. It goes without saying that they are completely absolved of any responsibility for the text at hand.

Finally, I would like to thank my family for their support and patience.

Carl Pedersen
Copenhagen, February 2009

Prologue: 27 July 2004

On 27 July 2004, just a little over two months after the fiftieth anniversary of the seminal Supreme Court decision on the case of *Brown* v. *Board of Education* that overturned a 1896 ruling permitting segregation by declaring that separate educational institutions for African Americans and whites was inherently unconstitutional, an African American took the stage at the Democratic National Convention in Boston to deliver the keynote address. Barack Obama entered stage left to the upbeat tones of Curtis Mayfield's 'Keep on Pushing', a hit for The Impressions in 1964, the same year that President Lyndon B. Johnson signed the Civil Rights Act into law.

Obama was a virtually unknown state senator from Illinois who was running for a seat in the US Senate. His advisers had lobbied the Democratic National Committee for a prominent speaking role for their candidate at the Convention. The party's presidential nominee, Senator John Kerry of Massachusetts, had met Obama several times and they had appeared together at a rally on the West Side of Chicago. Kerry was impressed with Obama's rhetorical skills, which were in marked contrast to Kerry's own, more wooden style. At Kerry's urging, Obama was offered the keynote speech on Tuesday evening. In 2000, the keynote had been delivered by another promising young African American politician, Harold Ford, Jr of Tennessee. Ford would go on to narrowly lose his own senatorial race in 2006 and instead, the following year, he became the head of the Democratic Leadership Council formerly run by Bill Clinton. Despite Ford's promise, his Convention speech failed to energize the crowd, in part because it was heavily edited by the Democratic National Committee. Obama, who had published an autobiography, *Dreams from My Father*, which was widely praised not only for its content but its lucid and elegant prose, insisted on writing the speech himself.

His speech electrified the Convention. Drawing on his autobiography, Obama made a conscious decision to interweave what he saw as his own improbable story with the larger and familiar American story.

Six years after the Declaration of Independence and one year before the signing of the Treaty of Paris that ended the American Revolution, a French immigrant with the rather grandiloquent name J. Hector St. John de Crèvecoeur wrote a book with the humble title *Letters from an American Farmer* – a collection of missives from an imaginary American farmer of English descent and self-styled 'simple cultivator of the earth', to 'gratify the curiosity of a friend' in his home country. In the third letter Crèvecoeur, in the guise of an unassuming farmer, took it upon himself to offer a succinct definition of 'the American, this new man'. The American was 'either an European, or the descendant of an European, hence that strange mixture of blood, which you will find in no other country'. He went on to describe the 'march of the Europeans toward the interior parts of this continent', from the coastal regions infused by maritime commerce, through the middle settlements purified by the cultivation of the soil, to the sparsely populated frontier where settlers relived the beginning of the European presence. This mix and movement were the mark of the American at the end of the eighteenth century, ready to build a new nation.[1]

Obama was an American for the twenty-first century. If current immigration trends continue unabated, by mid-century the United States will, according to estimates from the Census Bureau, no longer consist of a majority of descendents of European immigrants and will instead be comprised of a majority of Asians, Africans, Middle Easterners and

Latin Americans and their descendents. Census figures from 2000 revealed a distinct rise in the number of Americans of mixed race, so Obama's background is perhaps not as 'unlikely' as he would make it out to be. That being said, there was an aura of uniqueness in the story of this, as he put it, 'skinny kid with a funny name'.[2]

Obama is the son of a white mother from the American heartland with roots in Ireland and of a father from the Luo ethnic group in Kenya. He thus embodies both the old immigration from Europe that Crèvecoeur referred to and the new immigration from outside of Europe that is a feature of the twenty-first century.

His parents journeyed as far West as possible, to the youngest state, Hawaii. Obama grew up in the only state that had from the beginning been a majority–minority state. In his speech, he praised the diversity of the United States and its tradition of individualism, but reminded his audience of another tradition, that of community and solidarity, based on the Biblical principle, 'I am my brother's keeper.' This sense of community was enshrined in the motto of the United States, *e pluribus unum*: out of many, one.

The audience was brought to its feet with the lines that rejected the partisan bickering and divisiveness that had been a feature of the past decades and that went against the spirit of *e pluribus unum*: 'There is not a liberal America and a conservative America – there is the United States of America. There is not a black America and a white America and Latino America and Asian America – there's the United States of America.' He roundly dismissed the spurious division of the US into red and blue states by arguing that people living in the blue states could well be devoutly religious and those living in the red states might well have gay friends. Obama was consciously constructing a vision of a post-partisan and post-racial United States for the twenty-first century.

The speech immediately garnered much comment, most

of it positive. As the crowd rose up in appreciation, journalists scrambled to assess the impact of the speech. Perhaps one of the most incisive pieces of commentary came from the PBS broadcast *The News Hour with Jim Lehrer*. Lehrer was in a booth high above the convention with regular guests David Brooks of the *New York Times* and syndicated columnist Mark Shields. Brooks was quick to characterize the speech as 'a bit of history' and lamented that the major networks had decided not to cover the Convention that evening. He noted (presumably with some satisfaction) that Obama struck some socially conservative notes. Shields concurred and quoted passages from the speech in which Obama argued that government alone could not provide uplift and responsibility for inner-city youth. As Obama put it, 'parents have to parent . . . children can't achieve unless we raise their expectations and turn off the television sets and eradicate the slander that says a black youth with a book is acting white.'[3] Perhaps Obama was recalling another recent speech that spoke of parental responsibility and the need for education and uplift. The comedian Bill Cosby had surprised his audience at the NAACP Commemoration of the fiftieth anniversary of *Brown* by launching into a tirade against what Juan Williams has called 'the culture of failure' in Black America. 'In the neighborhood that most of us grew up in, parenting is not going on,' Cosby charged. He excoriated black youth for 'fighting to be ignorant' and concluded angrily, 'What the hell good is Brown v Board of Education if nobody wants it?'[4]

All three commentators were clearly impressed by Obama's eloquence and delivery and the message of unity he sounded. Indeed, Brooks distinguished the conciliatory tenor of Obama's message from the presumably more divisive, or 'old' Democratic, rhetoric of Howard Dean, John Kerry and John Edwards.

The threesome were then joined by historian Robert Norton Smith, the director of the Abraham Lincoln

Presidential Library and Museum in Springfield, Illinois. Lehrer, obviously taken with Obama's composure and self-assurance, asked Smith if Obama often put on the same kind of performance in his home state. Smith replied that Obama had been a rising star for some time in Illinois and that people there were already talking of him as the first black president.

The idea of an African American president was not new. In May 1961, only months after the first Catholic president was inaugurated, Robert F. Kennedy, in a Voice of America broadcast, claimed that 'in the next forty years a Negro can achieve the same position that my brother has'. In popular culture, Americans have long been used to seeing an African American, whether it be Morgan Freeman in the film *Deep Impact* or Dennis Haysbert in the TV series *24*, leading the nation with a steady hand in a time of crisis.

Forty years had passed and Obama at the time of his speech had not even won the Senate election in Illinois. In November, Kerry lost the presidential election, but Obama won his Senate seat by a landslide. He received 70 per cent of the vote against 27 per cent for his Republican opponent, Alan Keyes.

Obama's political skills and charisma were not the only reason for his overwhelming victory, however. Keyes was a particularly weak opponent. An African American former ambassador (and sometime presidential candidate), Keyes was ultra-conservative and something of a loose cannon. The Grand Old Party, or GOP (the name often given to the Republican Party) had chosen Keyes after Jack Ryan, who was running a strong campaign against Obama, was felled by a sex scandal. Keyes was only able to run after he moved from his native Maryland and took up residence in Illinois, which did little to alter the public perception of him as a carpetbagger.

Obama became the fifth African American elected to the US Senate, and only the third since Reconstruction. His two immediate predecessors, Edward Brooke, a Republican from Massachusetts, and Carol Moseley Braun, a Democrat from Illinois, were elected in 1967 and 1993 respectively. However, the odds against a viable African American candidate for president might still have seemed insurmountable. Since the end of the Civil Rights movement, African Americans had achieved success in politics mostly at the local level – primarily as mayors of major cities. Indeed, the election of Harold Washington as mayor of Chicago in 1983 was an inspiration to Obama, who moved that same year to take a low-paying job as a community organizer in the same South Side area where Washington came from. The first African American governor, Douglas Wilder of Virginia, was only elected in 1990.

Shirley Chisholm had made a run for president in 1972 – the first woman and African American to do so, but ended up with a paltry 151.95 votes at the Convention. Jesse Jackson had more success in the 1980s. In 1984, he won five primaries and caucuses, and in 1988, eleven contests. At the 1988 Democratic Convention, Jackson received a total of 1,219 delegate votes and came in second to the party's nominee, Governor Michael Dukakis of Massachusetts. Former Senator Carol Moseley Braun entered the race in 2003, but dropped out before the Iowa caucuses. In 2004, Baptist minister and Civil Rights activist Al Sharpton ran his presidential campaign until March. However, his candidacy garnered little media attention and even less support.

Unlike these African American candidates, Obama did not come out of the Civil Rights movement. He was born in 1961, the same year that Robert F. Kennedy made his prediction that an African American could be elected president by the beginning of the twenty-first century. He belonged to a new generation of African American politicians, along with Harold Ford, Jr, Deval Patrick, the current governor of Massachusetts, and Cory Booker, the mayor of Newark, New Jersey.

Prologue

In the wake of his convincing win for the US Senate, Obama had to fend off speculation that he was planning to run for president. In early 2007, however, he felt that his time had come. He had stayed in the spotlight since his 2004 Convention speech. In 2006, he published his second book, *The Audacity of Hope*, in which he outlined his political philosophy and recounted his first years as a senator.

Towards the end of the book, Obama revealed how he often jogged past the famous Washington monuments and stopped at the Lincoln memorial. He would read the Gettysburg Address and the Second Inaugural Address and gaze out over the reflecting pool, standing on the steps where Martin Luther King, Jr delivered his most famous speech in August 1963. His sense of wonder at those who had gone before him and achieved so much was reminiscent of another fledgling politician, this one from the world of film.[5]

In Frank Capra's *Mr. Smith Goes to Washington*, a wide-eyed and innocent Jefferson Smith comes to the nation's capital as a political novice, chosen to replace a senator in an unnamed south-western state who has suddenly died. It being 1939, Smith does not jog, but takes a bus past the same monuments that Obama gazed at more than half a century later. Smith stops at the Lincoln Memorial. His eyes wander from the inscribed texts of Lincoln's Second Inaugural Address and the Gettysburg Address. He overhears a boy standing nearby reading the line about 'a new birth of freedom' from the Gettysburg Address as an elderly African American approaches the statue of Lincoln. The link between the Founding Fathers and the American Everyman is reflected in Smith's first name and surname, and Lincoln provides the proper inspiration as a man of integrity and principle (and yes, inexperience, having only served two years in the Illinois State Assembly before becoming president). By the end of the film, the naive Smith, tempered in the ways of Washington, lives up to Lincoln's legacy by standing up to the corrupt politicians who have subverted the ideals of American democracy.

In a moment fraught with symbolism, another Illinoisan, now a US senator, but only recently in the Illinois State Assembly, chose to begin his campaign for president on the grounds of the Capitol Building in Springfield, Illinois, where Lincoln delivered his 'House Divided' speech that launched his failed campaign for US Senate in 1858. The symbolism was not lost on Obama. He evoked Lincoln several times, using the phrase 'a house divided' as a warning, emphasizing Lincoln's mission of uniting a nation divided by slavery, and calling for a renewal of this idea of one America to meet the challenges of the twenty-first century.

Obama also offered more of his autobiography, telling the large crowd that had gathered in below-freezing temperatures of his work in Chicago as a community organizer and constitutional lawyer. He linked his work to the idea of 'reclaiming the meaning of citizenship, restoring our sense of common purpose'.

The tenor of his speech recalled that of another president – John F. Kennedy. In his inaugural address in 1961, JFK noted that, with his election, 'the torch had been passed to a new generation'. Obama was born that same year and strictly speaking was part of the Baby Boom generation. But he clearly saw himself as closer to the post-Baby Boom generations that were too young to remember the Civil Rights movement and now lived in a society that, if not post-racial, had rejected segregation. These generations were too young to remember Vietnam (and were disinterested in the attacks on John Kerry's Vietnam War record in 2004), but had absorbed its significance by opposing the War in Iraq.

Obama made note of his own view of the war, saying that he was against it 'from the start', an oblique reference to a speech delivered in October 2002 in which he forcefully stated his opposition to an impending war which he regarded as 'dumb' and 'rash' and based 'not on principle but on politics'.[6] His steadfast opposition to the war would provide a stark contrast to his main opponents in the primaries, Hillary Clinton and John Edwards, both of whom voted for the 2002 Congressional resolution authorizing President George W. Bush to go to war with Iraq in 2003. He emphasized the need to rebuild alliances after Bush's failed unilateral foreign policy. During the campaign for the Democratic nomination, he would further distance himself from Bush administration policies by expressing a willingness to enter into dialogue with hostile nations such as Venezuela and Iran.

Obama ended his Convention speech on a high note. As Martin Luther King, Jr evoked Lincoln's Gettysburg Address at the beginning of his 'I Have a Dream' speech in 1963, Obama closed by citing one of the most important phrases of that most famous of Lincoln's speeches. In speaking of the need for a 'new birth of freedom', Obama harked back to the dark days of the Civil War and the words that contributed to the transformation of the carnage at Gettysburg to a renewal of the American promise, implying that he desired the same for the twenty-first century.

Obama left the stage to the sound of Jackie Wilson's forty-year-old soul hit 'Higher and Higher'.

Part One
Obama's America

1

Identities

Two versions of what it means to be American in the twenty-first century were articulated as part of the rhetorical strategy of the presidential campaign of 2008. One is a backlash national identity that emerged in the wake of the Civil Rights movement, the changes in immigration law and the rise of identity politics in the 1960s and 70s. It is socially conservative, largely white and conservative Christian, and finds its strength in nonurban areas of the US. It defines national identity in terms of Samuel Huntington's nostalgic, neonativist, and narrow view of an Anglo-Protestant culture. The other version, often derided as elitist, is an emergent national identity for the twenty-first century. It is progressive, includes African Americans and new minorities with a sizeable component of non-Christians, and is strongest in metropolitan areas of the US. This national identity is more cosmopolitan and transnational in nature.

The paradox of the election of 2008 is that the former, despite shrinking numbers, dominated political discourse, while the latter, demographically on the ascendent, found itself stigmatized as being outside the mainstream.

As the first nonwhite presidential candidate of a major political party, Barack Obama was representative of the coming transformation of American national identity in the twenty-first century. Yet Obama's identity became an issue in the presidential campaign. He was forced to counter characterizations that he was, in essence, a stranger, a sojourner with no fixed identity from the 'exotic' state of Hawaii.

Obama, far from being less than American, reflects the social, cultural and demographic developments that are transforming the US in the twenty-first century. Speakers at the Republican National Convention in St Paul may have lauded the virtues of small-town America, but that narrative of an idealized past represents a rapidly shrinking populace.

American presidential elections, it has been said, are quadrennial plebiscites on national identity.[1] The election of 2008 was no exception. For the past eight years, the nation had been governed by the first Southern conservative president since James Polk was elected in 1844. George W. Bush's political ancestors, according to Michael Lind, 'are not the Southern presidents of the twentieth century, but reactionary Southern senators and representatives who dominated the Democratic Party from the early nineteenth century until the New Deal, and who took over the Republican Party in the 1990s'.[2]

In 2008, the US was faced with the prospect of not only the first African American president, but someone who was the son of a lapsed Muslim from Kenya and a white atheist from the American heartland, who was born in the only US state detached from the North American continent and who had spent part of his childhood in the largest Muslim society in the world. Barack Obama's background was in many respects the diametrical opposite of George W. Bush's. Bush could feel comfortable in what Rick Perlstein has called Nixonland, an America based on the 'notion that there are two kinds of Americans', the one the middle-class Silent Majority, the other liberal cosmopolitans.[3]

In this strange country, Obama became the ultimate stranger. The Republican Party (and, it must be said, advisers to the campaign of Democratic candidate Senator Hillary Clinton of New York) decided to use the politics of identity as a campaign strategy. Obama was to be cast as a stranger in Republican America.

The great irony of the election of 2008 is that the Republicans, who were convinced they represented the 'real' America, were in reality the party of an ever-shrinking base. Obama, the so-called stranger and elusive personality, was in reality a figure who represented what it means to be American in the twenty-first century.

Who is Barack Obama?

'Who is Barack Obama?' The question was posed by Republican presidential candidate Senator John McCain of Arizona at numerous rallies in the waning days of the 2008 campaign. McCain's running mate, Sarah Palin, the governor of Alaska, joined in with unabashed enthusiasm by implying that there was something suspect about Obama's view of the United States. At a fundraiser in Denver, Colorado in October, Palin characterized Obama as 'not a man who sees America as you see America and as I see America'. In the spirit of Nixonland, Palin and her most fervent supporters proceeded to construct a nation divided into 'real' America and something vaguely anti-American.

Virginia was a good example. According to McCain adviser Nancy Pfotenhauer, the southwestern corner of the state was populated by 'real' Americans while northern Virginia had become part of metro DC. In 2004, Obama had laid out a vision of a united America that would end the division between red and blue states. In 2008, the Republicans seemed intent on maintaining an America forever divided between urban and rural, north and south, nationalist and cosmopolitan.

In keeping with his emphasis on a more cohesive national identity, Obama made a conscious decision to adopt

Howard Dean's fifty-state strategy to make the Democratic Party competitive in as many sections of the country as possible. In contrast, the Republicans elected to run on the politics of division that Richard Nixon had used to great effect in 1968 and that had characterized Republican electoral strategy ever since. In 2008, this policy was doomed to fail, not least because of the profound demographic changes that had taken place in the previous forty years. Since 1992, the Republicans had won the popular vote in only one presidential election.

According to *New York Times* columnist David Brooks, Obama had himself contributed to lingering doubts about his identity. In an op-ed column in August 2008, 'Where's the Landslide?', Brooks wondered why Obama wasn't doing better in his contest with McCain. He argued that voters were 'wary and uncertain' of Obama because they were confused about his identity. Brooks noted that Obama had chosen as the epigraph to his autobiography a Biblical passage from the book of Chronicles: 'For we are strangers before thee, and sojourners, as were all our fathers.' Obama's wanderings had unmoored him from any fixed identity. He was, in Brooks's view, unattached, difficult to pin down.

This has been a consistent pattern throughout his odyssey. His childhood was a peripatetic journey through Kansas, Indonesia, Hawaii and beyond. He absorbed things from those diverse places but was not fully of them.[4]

In the preface to the 2004 edition of *Dreams from My Father*, Obama offered a different take on the salience of his background. He expressed his firm belief that the story of his family 'might speak in some way to the fissures of race that have characterized the American experience, as well as the fluid state of identity . . . that mark our modern life'.[5]

His narrative was a testament to a multifaceted background that was composed of what the Indian economist and philosopher Amartya Sen has characterized as competing identities. In *Identity and Violence*, Sen argues that the kind of rigid categorization that confines national identity to religion or 'civilizations' ignores the range of other identities that people hold dear. This wilful 'miniaturization' of identity establishes false boundaries that are then defended at any cost. It is only by acknowledging that each individual possesses a multiplicity of identities that violence predicated on the fervent belief in rigid demarcations of groups according to ethnic belonging and/or religious affiliation can be abrogated.[6]

In order to break the impasse of basing identity on destiny, Sen emphasizes the element of choice in the construction of individual identity. Obama's autobiography attests to his recognition that, as the biracial son of a man from Kenya and woman from Kansas growing up in Hawaii, his life has been a series of choices about who he is. Both Sen and Obama see this construction of identity as a feature of contemporary life that is often wilfully denied in political discourse.

Bent on portraying the Democratic frontrunner as the ultimate stranger, the Republicans were all too eager to construct their own miniaturization of Obama's identity, based on innuendo and falsehoods. In Sen's terms, the Republicans and their surrogates in the media took his complex identity and incarcerated it within the narrow confines of caricature.

During the course of the campaign of 2008, Obama was branded as a Muslim because, it was falsely alleged, he had attended an Indonesian *madrassa*. A video showing Obama with his hands clasped in front of him while the national anthem was being played was used to stamp him as unpatriotic. He was accused of harbouring the same hateful views of the pastor of his church, the Trinity United Church of Christ, the Reverend Jeremiah Wright, who in a number of sermons, excerpts of which were circulated

on the Internet, exhorted his audience with incendiary pronouncements like 'God damn America!'. Obama was linked
to William Ayers, a professor at the College of Education
at the University of Illinois in Chicago, who in his younger
days was a founding member of the notorious radical left-
wing group the Weather Underground, which had carried
out a series of bombings in the early 1970s. The supposed
association between Obama and Ayers was, however, more
benign than the GOP cared to admit. Between 1999 and
2002, Obama and Ayers served on the board of an anti-
poverty organization, the Woods Fund of Chicago. As
Obama pointed out, he was only a boy when the Weather
Underground was engaged in its violent acts. Not content
to paint him as an unpatriotic Muslim with ties to domestic
terrorism, the Republicans in the last weeks of the campaign
resorted to calling Obama a socialist, or, as McCain would
have it, 'the great redistributor'.

In July, *The New Yorker* ran a cover that attempted to sum
up the construction of Obama's identity by his opponents.
The cover, entitled 'The Politics of Fear', depicted Barack
and Michelle Obama in the White House, he in Muslim
garb (no doubt inspired by a widely circulated photo of
Obama wearing traditional clothing, taken during a trip to
the Kenyan border with Somalia and Ethiopia in 2006), she
resembling a latter-day Black Panther, replete with bushy
Afro, military garb and machine gun slung over her shoul-
der. They are celebrating their good fortune of achieving
the White House with the militant fist bump they had first
unveiled for the public after Obama had effectively won the
Democratic nomination in early June. A portrait of Osama
bin Laden hangs over the mantelpiece and the American
flag is burning in the fireplace. The Other has become
president.[7]

During the course of the campaign, Obama and his
supporters were continually forced to address questions
about his identity. So persistent was the onslaught on his

Identities

identity that the Obama campaign managers felt compelled to launch a website, 'Fight the Smears', designed to debunk the various allegations cast upon their candidate.[8] The Republicans living in Nixonland could therefore only construct an identity for Obama that perpetuated the notion of two Americas. Obama's task was more difficult. He had to counter the Republican narrative of American identity that had dominated political discourse for the better part of forty years with a new narrative, one that reflected the demographic changes that augured a new American identity for the twenty-first century.

Believing Obama

Persistent rumours that Obama was in fact a Muslim were fuelled not only by stories that he had attended a *madrassa* while living in Indonesia, but by the photograph of Obama in Muslim garb.[9] During the primary campaign, Hillary Clinton, in a wide-ranging interview on the CBS news programme *60 Minutes*, fielded questions from Steve Kroft on Obama's religious beliefs. While she made it clear that she did not think Obama was a Muslim, at one point she added 'as far as I know' which prompted *New York Times* columnist Bob Herbert to characterize her comments as 'one of the sleaziest moments of the campaign to date'.[10]

After Obama won the Democratic nomination in June, the *New Yorker* cover renewed interest in his religious affiliation. A Pew survey taken in July found that 12 per cent believed Obama was a Muslim.[11] Right-wing pundits and talk-show hosts contributed to keeping alive rumours of Obama as Muslim. In a book released only weeks before Obama's inauguration, *Guilty: Liberal 'Victims' and Their Assault on America*, the notorious right-wing scribe Ann Coulter referred to Obama as B. Hussein Obama in order to highlight his purported connection to Islam.

It fell to an African American Republican to offer what

19

was perhaps the most eloquent refutation of the characterization of Obama as Muslim. A few weeks before the election, Obama received the endorsement of Colin Powell, the former Secretary of State in the Bush administration. Appearing on the NBC Sunday morning broadcast *Meet the Press* on 19 October, Powell explained at length why he had after much deliberation decided to support Obama, characterizing him as a potential 'transformative' president. Powell's endorsement was all the more poignant because of his own identity as an African American son of Jamaican immigrants. In the mid-1990s, Powell was the subject of much speculation as to whether he would run for president in 1996. In November 1995 he announced that he was a Republican, but would not seek the nomination of his party for president. He did, however, address the 1996 Convention. His speech was curiously out of sync with the direction of the party, especially after the Gingrich revolution of 1994. Powell reminded the delegates that the GOP was the party of Lincoln and must therefore 'always be the party of inclusion'. His appeal for a party of the big tent was unrequited.

Twelve years later, Powell assessed the record of his party and found it wanting. He criticized the 'narrow' approach of the Republicans and, echoing the theme of his 1996 speech, praised Obama's 'more inclusive, broader reach into the needs and aspirations of our people'.

The notion that Obama was a Muslim or at least something un-American produced some embarrassing moments for the McCain campaign. At one rally in Minnesota in October 2008, a woman from the audience, clearly confused about Obama's identity, confronted McCain with a halting description of the Democratic presidential candidate as 'an Arab'. McCain received a good deal of praise for immediately dispelling the notion that Obama was an 'Arab' by saying that 'he is a decent family man' (as if the two were mutually exclusive).[12]

Powell addressed this characterization on *Meet the Press*. He pointed out that denying that Obama was a Muslim (or Arab for that matter) was not a proper response. 'Is there something wrong with being a Muslim in this country?' Powell mused and then continued, 'The answer's no, that's not America.' He went on to ask whether a Muslim child should not be able to have the same aspirations to the US presidency one day as any other American.[13]

Obama's religious affiliation was in fact more complex than the widespread misperception that he was a Muslim or the simple rejoinder that he was a Christian. Obama joined the Trinity United Church of Christ in Chicago in 1987. During his childhood, however, he had been exposed to both secularism and a range of religious beliefs. According to a schoolfriend Obama's mother, Stanley Ann Dunham, was an atheist.[14] His father, Barack Obama, Sr, was raised a Muslim, but had become an atheist by the time he married Obama's mother. His Indonesian stepfather, Lolo Soetero, was a moderate Muslim who incorporated animism, Buddhism and Hinduism in his religious worldview.[15] In Indonesia Obama attended a Roman Catholic elementary school and a state-run school, and was also home-schooled by his mother. His grandparents, who raised him in Hawaii, came from Methodist and Baptist denominations in the Mid-West, but had largely forsaken their religious roots. They passed on this skepticism to their daughter.

Obama described his eclectic religious background this way:

I was not raised in a religious household . . . For my mother, organized religion too often dressed up close-mindedness in the garb of piety, cruelty and oppression in the cloak of righteousness.

This isn't to say that she provided me with no religious instruction. In her mind, a working knowledge of the world's great religions was a necessary part of any well-rounded education. In our household the Bible, the Koran, and the Bhagavad Gita sat on the shelf alongside books of Greek and Norse and African mythology. On Easter or Christmas Day, my mother might drag me to church, just as she dragged me to the Buddhist temple, the Chinese New Year celebration, the Shinto shrine, and ancient Hawaiian burial sites.[16]

As a counterpoint to the rumours that he was a Muslim, Obama announced shortly after the election that he would use his full name – Barack Hussein Obama – at his inauguration. Even though he made it clear that he did not intend to 'make a statement' and was merely following custom, if not protocol – Ronald Reagan chose not to use his middle name of Wilson when he was inaugurated – the inclusion of his middle name, seen in the context of how the right was using it to link him to Islam, sent a signal of outreach and reconciliation.

In that spirit, Obama also announced that he would give a 'major policy address' in a Muslim capital shortly after his inauguration. Not surprisingly, Jakarta was mentioned as a possible site, as were Cairo and Ankara.

Conservatives often refer to the US as a Christian nation. In an interview with the spiritual website Beliefnet during the campaign, McCain stated unequivocally that 'the Constitution established the United States of America as a Christian nation'.[17] Since Ronald Reagan's first campaign in 1980, when he assured evangelical Christians that even though they could not endorse him, he endorsed them, they have been among the most fervent supporters of the Republicans. Even though Obama made slight inroads into this group, the overwhelming majority of those identifying themselves as evangelical Christians voted for McCain (72 per cent to 26 per cent). Obama, however, did better than the 2004 Democratic presidential nominee John Kerry among virtually every other group. His total vote among all religious voters was 53 per cent to McCain's 46 per cent, a five-point increase over Kerry's showing in 2004.[18]

Obama's exposure to a number of religions and his shifting religious identity arguably made him more conscious and tolerant of the growing diversity of religion in America in the decades following the 1965 Immigration Act. As Diana Eck has observed, the paradox of modern America is that while conservative Christian groups have become more vocal, the emergence of 'the most religiously diverse nation on earth' has been largely hidden from view.[19] A recent survey found that 'religious affiliation in the U.S. is both very diverse and extremely fluid'.[20] Those identifying themselves as adherents of 'other faiths', which include the new religions Eck discusses, voted for Obama by a margin comparable to that which McCain received from evangelicals (73 per cent to 22 per cent).[21]

The demographics of identity

Suspicions of Obama's tenuous ties to the US extended even to his place of birth. Appearing on the ABC Sunday programme *This Week*, NPR news analyst and ABC political commentator Cokie Roberts questioned the wisdom of Obama's decision to spend his summer vacation in Hawaii. Assuring her listeners that she was of course aware that Hawaii is a state, Roberts nevertheless chided Obama for spending time there, because it simply 'has the look' of 'going off to some foreign, exotic place'. A better choice, according to Roberts, would be Myrtle Beach, South Carolina (a place that Palin would surely regard as a 'pro-American' area of the country).[22]

By coincidence, the Democratic candidate for president and the Republican candidate for vice president came from the last two states to enter the union. The contrast between Hawaii and Alaska could not be more stark.[23] In 1893 Hawaii was the first territory to be subject to US regime

23

change, five years before the start of the Spanish–American War.[24] It remains the only state in the US that has had a majority–minority population since statehood. Its distance from the mainland and its tropical climate make the archipelago seem, like Obama, somehow not of the US. Alaska was acquired from Russia in 1867. It promotes itself as the Last Frontier, a bastion of the kind of rugged America that historian Frederick Jackson Turner, speaking in 1893, the year of the overthrow of the Hawaiian government, argued was no more. Palin was presented as a true representative of the Alaskan ethos: a former mayor of a small town who enjoyed hunting and advocated drilling in the Arctic National Wildlife Refuge to help make the US independent of foreign oil.

The paradox of the demographics of identity that played out in 2008 was epitomized in the difference between the two last states to enter the union. With its polyglot population, Hawaii resembled the American future. Alaska, in promoting itself as the repository of the frontier spirit, was a throwback to the American past.

The US, at the beginning of the twenty-first century, is in transition. Current trends of immigration portend that more and more states will soon resemble Hawaii, rather than Alaska. Seven years before the dawn of the twentieth century, Frederick Jackson Turner had attempted to define the national character for a new age in which the continental frontier had been settled. Eight years after the start of the twenty-first century, Obama represented an emergent new America.

Not only were Obama's 'exotic' origins in Hawaii suspect, but his childhood and youth were marked by a degree of itinerancy. He lived in Hawaii, then Indonesia, then returned to Hawaii. He left Hawaii to go to Occidental College in California, attended law school at Harvard and then moved to New York City. In 1985, however, he came to Chicago, the third largest city in the US, and has lived there ever since.

In contrasting their America with the one that Obama purportedly represented, the McCain/Palin campaign reached back into the past. Making her first major speech at the Republican National Convention in St Paul, Minnesota on 3 September, Palin conjured up the image that for her best described what America was all about. As she put it, 'A writer observed: "We grow good people in our small towns, with honesty, sincerity, and dignity."'[25] Her praise of small towns elicited a rapturous response from the almost exclusively white audience. Apparently unbeknown to her (but certainly not to her speechwriters), the 'writer' she quoted was none other than Westbrook Pegler, whom a reporter-researcher at the *New Republic* characterized as an 'ultraconservative newspaper columnist whose widely syndicated columns (at its peak, 200 newspapers and 12 million readers) targeted the New Deal establishment, labor leaders, intellectuals, homosexuals, Jews, and poets.'[26] Palin elaborated on her vision of small-town America on the campaign trail. For her, the small towns scattered across the nation represented not only the 'real' America, they were 'pro-America areas of this great nation'.[27] A little-known Republican member of the House from Minnesota, Michele Bachmann, was so persuaded by Palin's remarks that she called for newspapers to launch an investigation into 'anti-American' members of Congress, including Obama.[28] If Bachmann thought that her revival of the McCarthyite witch-hunting of the 1950s would resonate with her constituents, she was sorely mistaken. She won re-election only by a small margin.

The focus on small-town America was a rather transparent campaign tactic to appeal directly to the Republican base. Palin herself was the perfect representative of the idea that the true identity of the US could be found in small towns. She had been mayor of Wasilla, Alaska at a time when the population was just over 5,000. Indeed, her choice as McCain's running mate fitted in well with her demographic background. What could be more quintessentially American than a small town in a sparsely populated state that liked to market itself as the Last Frontier? In this sense Palin possessed, in the eyes of the core Republican constituencies, a certain Little House on the Prairie quality – a small community sustaining traditional American values and infused by the frontier spirit. Never mind that Alaska, with its vast federal lands and its pork-barrel politics, was in many respects the obverse of the 'real' America which Palin shamelessly promoted.

It was precisely this carefully honed image, designed to appeal to white rural voters, that proved the undoing of the McCain/Palin ticket at the polls on 4 November 2008. The supreme irony of the election of 2008 was that the campaign that ran on the slogan 'Country First' constructed a 'real' America that no longer existed and ultimately lost to a campaign that garnered support from the growing metropolitan areas of the US. The small towns and rural areas that became a staple of McCain's and especially Palin's rhetoric on the campaign trail are hardly representative of the US in the twenty-first century. The idea of small-town America is a holdover from a distant past. The last time that most Americans still lived in rural areas of the country was in 1910, according to the Census Bureau. By 1920, largely as a result of immigration and internal migration, that was no longer the case and the Census of that year showed, for the first time in American history, that more Americans lived in cities than in rural areas. The 1920s saw the emergence of a rural backlash against urban America that expressed itself in renewed nativist sentiment, attacks on the teaching of Darwinism in public schools and the resurgence of the Ku Klux Klan. In the twenty-first century, a full 84 per cent of Americans live in the 363 metropolitan areas of the US defined by the Census Bureau as cities with a population of 50,000 or more, interdependent with outlying suburbs.[29] The attempt to link American identity with the

demographic anachronism of small-town America constituted the last gasp of a backlash against the reality of metropolitan America in the twenty-first century.

Even on a superficial level, the contrast between the
Republican vision of who we are and the identity of the
Democratic presidential candidate was striking. Unlike
Alaska, the archipelago of Obama's birth is unattached to
the North American continent. Alaska is overwhelmingly
white, apart from a sizeable Alaskan native population.
Hawaii, on the other hand, is the first of now four majority–
minority states (with New Mexico, California and Texas)
with five states – Maryland, Mississippi, Georgia, New
York and Arizona – soon to follow, according to Census
Bureau estimates. The dispersal of especially Latino popu-
lations has contributed to making 10 per cent of all US counties majority–minority as of 2008.[30] Wasilla was perhaps the
closest the Republicans could come to the small towns of
yore.

Chicago, where Obama had moved in 1985, is the third
largest city in the US after New York and Los Angeles. It is
the diametrical opposite of small-town America. With 2.7
million residents, Chicago has four times the population of
the entire state of Alaska and ten times the population of
its largest city, Anchorage. Chicago's multicultural population, almost evenly divided among the three major groups
(37 per cent white, 36 per cent African American, 28 per
cent Latino), makes Chicago an example of what the future
America will look like.

The patriot

At Tom Harkin's Annual Steak Fry in Iowa in September
2007, Obama was photographed in front of a giant American
flag with fellow Democratic candidates Governor Bill
Richardson of New Mexico and Hillary Clinton, during
the playing of the national anthem. While Richardson and

Clinton were shown with their right hand over their heart, Obama stood with his hands clasped in front of him. The photograph was first published in *Time* magazine and subsequently circulated on the Internet by various bloggers raising questions about Obama's patriotism. As Obama pointed out, his grandfather had taught him that it was only during the Pledge of Allegiance that putting your hand over your heart was called for, not during the playing of the national anthem.[31]

Long before the first vote was cast in Iowa, Obama was questioned about why he didn't wear a flag lapel pin. While campaigning in Iowa in October, 2007, a local ABC reporter asked why Obama chose not to wear a pin. Instead of tiptoeing around the issue, Obama confronted it head on:

> My patriotism speaks for itself. The truth is that right after 9/11, I had a pin. Shortly after 9/11, particularly because as we're talking about the Iraq war, that became a substitute for, I think, true patriotism, which is speaking out on issues that are of importance to our national security. I decided I won't wear that pin on my chest. Instead I'm going to try to tell the American people what I believe will make this country great and hopefully that will be a testimony to my patriotism.[32]

Obama was presenting a subtle argument that distinguished between purely symbolic expressions of patriotism and a patriotism that requires looking at the actions of a nation with a critical eye.

Obama's statement did not satisfy his opponents. He was in many respects operating at a disadvantage. The Republicans had long been casting Democratic candidates as less than loyal Americans. Since the Civil War and Reconstruction era, the Republicans had seen themselves as the party of 'legitimacy' and the embodiment of true American patriotism.[33] At the beginning of the twentieth century, the Democratic Party continued to be infiltrated with members and supporters who failed to fit into dominant conceptions of what it meant to be an American, best summed up by the charge that the Democrats were the party of 'rum, Romanism and rebellion' (as the adage from the election of 1884 went). The patriotism of these groups was brought into question by a variety of nativist groups and individuals. Anything less than the 100 per cent Americanism advocated by former President Theodore Roosevelt was deemed suspect.

Obama clearly felt that he could not ignore the narrative being promulgated by the Republicans that cast him as less than American and constantly called his patriotism into question. During the course of the campaign, he adopted a two-pronged approach in expressing his view of American patriotism. On the one hand, he expanded on his remarks in Iowa and articulated a patriotism that did not shy away from dissent and appealed to common sacrifice. On the other hand, he acquiesced to the conservative attacks. In the latter days of the campaign he took to wearing a flag lapel pin consistently and has done so since he was elected.

Furthermore, anxious to assure his countrymen that he was indeed one of them, Obama tailored his message to downtone the presumed exotic nature of his identity in favour of a more mainstream approach. The first ad of his general election campaign, 'The Country I Love', which aired in June, focused on his heartland Kansas roots. There was no reference to Hawaii or to his father.[34]

However, in a major speech on patriotism at the end of June in Independence, Missouri, the birthplace of President Harry S Truman, Obama made no attempt to conceal his upbringing in Hawaii and Indonesia and even went so far as to admit that he, as a young man, had 'no firm anchor in any particular community'. He acknowledged the importance of the debate over patriotism for American national identity by arguing that 'when we argue about patriotism, we are arguing about who we are as a country, and more importantly, who we should be'.[35]

The very essence of patriotism, according to Obama, was loyalty to American ideals and the recognition that if the US was not perfect, it could be made better through the active participation of an enlightened citizenry. Quoting the Missourian writer Mark Twain, Obama distinguished between always supporting the country, but only supporting the government when it deserved it.

Obama criticized the Bush administration for not living up to the ideal of patriotism by urging Americans to shop in the wake of 9/11 instead of calling upon Americans to sacrifice 'an imperative of citizenship'. Pointing to Martin Luther King, Jr fighting against racial injustice and a soldier speaking out against prisoner abuse at Abu Ghraib as true patriots, Obama expressed what patriotism meant to him:

> Recognizing a wrong being committed in this country's name; insisting that we deliver on the promise of our Constitution – these are the acts of patriots, men and women who are defending that which is best in America.[36]

At the Democratic Convention, Obama continued his concerted effort to counter the relentless portrayal of him as less than American, but toned down the rhetoric of his speech in Missouri. The biographical video that his wife Michelle introduced on the first day of the Convention was more in the vein of the narrative of the 'Country I Love' campaign ad than his Missouri speech. A fleeting image of Obama with his father was the extent of the video's focus on his African heritage. The video made much of Obama's heartland roots, referring to his maternal grandparents' hardships during the Depression and their contribution to the war effort – his grandfather fought in Patton's army and his grandmother worked at a bomber-assembly plant.

Identities

Even though the manufactured controversy over Obama's supposed reluctance to respect the flag and the conscious effort made by the Obama campaign to place him squarely within the American mainstream was apparent testimony to the salience of the Republican narrative, the question of Obama's exotic background and purported lack of patriotism turned out to have little effect at the voting booth.

A rooted cosmopolitan

Obama was criticized in some circles for traveling abroad in July 2008. His trip took him to Afghanistan, Iraq, Jordan, Israel, France, Britain and Germany. McCain dismissed his trip to the Middle East, apart from saying it was long overdue.

The European trip was of a different order. On 24 July, Obama greeted a crowd estimated at 200,000 at the Victory column in Berlin's Tiergarten Park. His appearance inevitably drew comparisons to two presidents. President John F. Kennedy uttered the famous (if grammatically incorrect) line 'Ich bin ein Berliner' at the Wall in 1963, only two years after it had been erected. President Ronald Reagan came to the Wall in 1987. Sensing a weakness in the Eastern bloc after the ascension of Mikhail Gorbachev to power in the Soviet Union in 1985, Reagan challenged him to 'tear down this Wall'.

Unlike Kennedy and Reagan, Obama came to Berlin not as president but as the Democratic nominee for president, a fact that elicited accusations of a certain presumptuousness on his part. More importantly, Obama came to a united Germany in the post-Cold War era. The title of his speech was revealing: 'A World that Stands as One', an obvious slight to the Bush administration's penchant for sowing discord with such nostrums as 'Either you are with us or you are with the terrorists' and 'Old and new Europe'.

Early on in the speech, Obama attempted to bond with his

foreign audience by unequivocally declaring that he came to Berlin as not only an American, but as 'a citizen of the world'.[37] Conservatives were quick to denounce Obama's one-worldism. George F. Will of the *Washington Post* warned that cosmopolitanism was 'not a political asset for American candidates', particularly for Obama, 'one of whose urgent needs is to seem comfortable with America's vibrant and very un-European patriotism, which is grounded in a sense of virtuous exceptionalism'. According to Will, the very definition of citizenship was 'legal and loyalty attachments to a particular political entity with a distinctive regime and culture'.[38]

The 'intertwined' world of the twenty-first century made it imperative that nations work together to bear 'the burdens of global citizenship', Obama argued. In an implicit critique of the Samuel Huntington notion of the inevitable clash of irreconcilable civilizations, Obama called for the tearing down of walls between allies, between rich and poor nations, between religions, and between natives and immigrants.[39]

Obama was implicitly rejecting the conservative view of citizenship articulated by Will. In many respects, the identity that Obama was attempting to formulate resembled that of rooted, or partial, cosmopolitanism. According to Kwame Anthony Appiah, who emigrated to the US from Ghana, the terms are emblematic of a twenty-first century-identity. In his book *Cosmopolitanism*, Appiah argues that

. . . we need take sides neither with the nationalist who abandons all foreigners nor with the hard-core cosmopolitan who regards her friends and fellow citizens with icy impartiality. The position worth defending might be called (in both senses) a partial cosmopolitanism.[40]

Between 1890 and 1920, a group of intellectuals including Jane Addams, John Dewey, W. E. B. Du Bois, Horace Kallen and Randolph Bourne attempted to formulate a counternarrative to dominant notions of imperial adventure, racism and nativism. These cosmopolitan patriots, as Jonathan Hansen has called them, promoted cultural diversity at home and critical engagement with US military adventures abroad.[41] In the first decades of the twentieth century, the cosmopolitan patriots were regarded as marginal and insignificant. By the beginning of the twenty-first century the idea of cosmopolitanism was still being contested. But in the debate between cosmopolitanism and nativism, the Republicans were fighting a losing battle.

By articulating a dual identity as an American citizen and a citizen of the world, Obama placed himself in the mould of the cosmopolitan patriots of the early twentieth century.

The redistributor

The notion that Obama was a socialist came after an exchange on taxes with Samuel Joseph Wurzelbacher – who came to be known as simply 'Joe the Plumber' – when he said, 'I think when you spread the wealth around, it's good for everybody.'[42] Joe the Plumber quickly emerged as the American Everyman and was co-opted by the McCain campaign. At one campaign rally, McCain introduced him only to discover that he was not present in the audience. McCain responded to Joe's absence by awkwardly declaring, 'You're all Joe the Plumber!'

The McCain campaign consciously tapped into a long-standing suspicion of 'socialism' as a state-controlled, un-American form of government that robbed citizens of their economic freedom. To underscore this message, the McCain campaign brought out someone who was born in Austria and thus grew up under one of these vaguely defined socialist systems. Just days before the election, the Republican governor of California, Arnold Schwarzenegger, told a McCain rally in Ohio: 'I left Europe four decades ago because socialism has killed opportunities there.'[43]

Never mind that a recent study by the London School of Economics showed that intergenerational social mobility is higher in Germany and the Nordic countries, all of whose social welfare systems were shaped by Social Democratic governments, than in the US.[44] The idea that Obama intended to institute socialist rule in the US, and that Joe the Plumber had got him to reveal his plans, was enough for the audience to express its disapproval.

In the election of 2008, the prospect of European social democracy contaminating the US was imminent, according to Republican conservatives. In July 2007 another Republican candidate who later dropped out of the race, former New York City mayor Rudolph Giuliani, gave this assessment of the proposals for health reform offered by the candidates for the Democratic presidential nomination:

> We've got to do it the American way. The American way is not single-payer, government-controlled anything. That's a European way of doing something; that's frankly a socialist way of doing something.[45]

Of all the Democratic candidates at the time, however, only Dennis Kucinich had proposed a single-payer health care system. Nevertheless, the implication of Giuliani's remarks was clear. Universal health care was predicated on government involvement. Increased government involvement was a capitulation to European socialism.

In the conservative Republican worldview, this had happened before. The US had always resisted succumbing to the threat of European socialism. And to be sure, there had been threats – from European immigrants coming to the US after the failed 1848 revolutions, from socialists and anarchists entering the US during the great wave of immigration from 1880 to 1920. The Red Scare of 1919 in the wake of the Bolshevik Revolution in Russia had been quashed by the US justice department. Joseph McCarthy had uncovered

Communist sympathizers at all levels of government in the 1940s. However, the resilience of the 'American way,' as Giuliani would have it, had provided a bulwark against the insidious intrusions of European socialism into the American body politic. Socialism was a foreign component completely at odds with American national identity. Karl Marx had often expressed the view that the US would likely become the first society to effect a socialist transformation because it had reached an advanced stage of capitalist development. However, even he and his associate Friedrich Engels acknowledged that conditions in the US might mitigate against a socialist revolution.[46] The German economist and sociologist Werner Sombart agreed. In 1906, he penned a treatise with the intriguing title *Warum gibt es in den Vereinigten Staaten keinen Sozialismus?* (Why Is There No Socialism in the United States?). His answer was simple: 'On roast beef and apple pie, all socialist utopias have gone to pot.'[47] American abundance trumped socialist agitation.

Until, that is, with the coming of the New Deal. The government activism of the New Deal era has long been a *bête noire* of Republican conservatism. As Steve Fraser and Gary Gerstle put it, 'When Ronald Reagan assumed office in January of 1981, an epoch in the nation's political history came to an end. The New Deal, as a dominant order of ideas, public policies, and political alliances, died, however much its ghost still hovers over a troubled polity.'[48] It is hardly surprising that Ronald Reagan, when he moved into the White House in early 1981, insisted on having a portrait of President Calvin Coolidge, guardian of the minimalist state, hung in the Cabinet Room. Seen in historical perspective, this gesture was replete with symbolism. It has been argued that presidents from Truman to Carter, including the Republicans Eisenhower and Nixon, in large measure either accepted the precepts of New

Deal liberalism or sought to expand it. It was after all the Republican president Richard Nixon who could claim in 1971 that 'We're all Keynesians now'. Reagan was in effect saying, we're done with the 1930s, it's time to go back to the 1920s.

This sentiment is at the heart of a revisionist history of the Depression era by Amity Shlaes, *The Forgotten Man*. Shlaes, a syndicated columnist for Bloomberg and former member of the editorial board of the *Wall Street Journal*, turns on its head the conventional narrative of 1920s rampant speculation leading to economic collapse in the 1930s and the New Deal saving capitalism by controlling its excesses. She rehabilitates Calvin Coolidge and Herbert Hoover, praising them for their support for laissez-faire capitalism and tax cuts. One chapter recounts a visit by a trade-union delegation including Rex Tugwell and Stuart Chase to the Soviet Union in 1927, where they were courted by Stalin and Trotsky and subsequently expressed admiration for the Soviet experiment. Tugwell and Chase were later to become top advisers to the Roosevelt administration and their enthusiasm for the benefits of economic planning influenced New Deal policies. Shlaes doesn't go so far as to stamp them as fellow-travellers. Rather, she accuses them of a kind of wilful gullibility:

> The problem was [the left New Dealers'] naïveté about the economic value of Soviet-style or European-style collectivism – and the fact they forced such collectivism on their own country.[49]

In spite of the best efforts of the McCain campaign, the characterization of Obama as an unrepentent socialist bent on resdistributing wealth had little resonance with the public. In the wake of the financial crisis, some form of government regulation was regarded by many Americans as a necessary step to recovery, not as creeping socialism.

Who are we?

These attempts to brand Obama as a rootless sojourner, a Muslim, an unpatriotic domestic subversive and a socialist agitator form part of an ongoing debate about American national identity. Speaking at the Republican National Convention in 1992, Patrick Buchanan, a leading cultural conservative who had challenged the sitting President George H. W. Bush for the Republican presidential nomination, reminded the assembled audience of the most important issue in the election:

> My friends, this election is about much more than who gets what. It is about who we are. It is about what we believe. It is about what we stand for as Americans. There is a religious war going on in our country for the soul of America. It is a cultural war, as critical to the kind of nation we will one day be as was the Cold War itself.[50]

A leading neoconservative went one step further. Irving Kristol contended that as soon as the Cold War between the United States and the Soviet Union ended in 1991, the 'real Cold War' had begun. The US, in Kristol's view, was singularly unprepared and vulnerable against the invidious enemy of the 'liberal ethos'.[51] By this measure, the chairwoman of the National Endowment for the Humanities, Lynne Cheney, was in the front line of this struggle. In what conservative columnist Charles Krauthammer had characterised as the 'unipolar moment' after the collapse of the Soviet Union, Lynne Cheney's job was arguably more important than that of her husband Dick, Secretary of Defense in George H. W. Bush's administration.

Samuel Huntington, author of the influential *Clash of Civilizations* which conceived of global geopolitics as a conflict between opposing belief systems, was similarly worried about the future of the US if immigration were to continue at current rates. His book on American national identity, *Who Are We?*, whose title echoed Buchanan's cultural call to arms, was an attempt to see American national identity as comprising an Anglo-Protestant cultural core that had been sustained over time. However, as Huntington pointed out, the resilience of this core was put to the test in the 1960s. Huntington links what he calls the 'decline in the centrality of national identity' with the rise of multiculturalism in the 1960s. The US was in danger of losing its core culture.[52]

Huntington feared that continued Mexican immigration and the consolidation of what he called subnational and transnational identitites, encouraged by business and political elites, would eat away at the core edifice of American national identity and eventually lead to the dissolution of the US nation state. For all its horror and trauma, the aftermath of 9/11 had witnessed a revival of nationalist spirit that could provide the cultural clue to holding the nation together in the face of forces that threatened to tear it asunder. Like Buchanan, Huntington believed that the very survival of the nation was at stake.

Elements within the conservative movement stoked this fear of the decline and fall of the US. Buchanan offered written fodder for the culture war, publishing books with ominous-sounding titles like *The Decline of the West* and *State of Emergency*. Republican presidential candidate Tom Tancredo, Republican House member from Colorado, ran a virtually one-issue campaign on his staunch opposition to further immigration from Mexico. His campaign was evidence of a split in the Republican Party. John McCain had, along with the liberal Senator Edward Kennedy, proposed an immigration bill that would provide a path to citizenship for the approximately 12 million undocumented immigrants living in the US. President Bush supported a path to citizenship, as did many businesses and influential newspapers such as the *Wall Street Journal*. Although his own campaign floundered, Tancredo succeeded in dominating the discussion on immigration before it faded from view in the presidential campaign. In one early debate, the Republican candidates nearly fell over themselves in scrambling to outdo Tancredo. McCain even refused to say if he would vote for his own bill. Commentator Lou Dobbs of CNN, however, has kept the flames of anti-immigration sentiment burning with his 'Broken Borders' segment. In the border region, members of the Minuteman Project vigilante group provide the foot soldiers for the anti-immigration movement.

Southern attitudes regarding the preservation of the purity of the races, necessitating their permanent separation, permeated the debates over immigration that took place in the first decades of the twentieth century. Nativist sentiment put pressure on Congress to stem the rising tide of immigration from Southern and Eastern Europe. In 1924, the Johnson–Reed Act effectively halted immigration. What John Higham has called a Nordic victory was in reality very much a Southern victory born of a desire to maintain a chimerical ethnic purity in a nation of immigrants.[53]

Whereas the prospect of miscegenation informed anxieties about black migration from South to North, religion and the spectre of socialism provided much of the impetus for anti-union sentiment. Anti-Catholicism had been a feature of nativist movements ever since the Irish came to American shores in the late 1840s and 1850s following the great potato famine. Their path to American identity was forged in large part by their feeling of innate superiority over those at the lowest rung of the American social ladder, African Americans. Given the persistence of these prejudices, it is worth noting that Obama's mother, Stanley Ann Dunham, was the descendent of Irish immigrants, who had to struggle to 'become white'.[54]

The colour line in the twenty-first century

Karl Rove, President George W. Bush's former top domestic adviser, liked to compare what he saw as the emergence of a new Republican majority in the twenty-first century to the election of 1896. Republican William McKinley beat his Democratic opponent William Jennings Bryan the same year as the Supreme Court decided in *Plessy* v. *Ferguson* that separate facilities for African Americans and whites was not inherently unequal. The decision gave the stamp of approval to efforts by the states of the former Confederacy to deny African Americans equal rights under the law. Two years later, the reconciliation between North and South took on another dimension. As part of the imperial moment launched by McKinley, troops from the North and South fought together against a common enemy in the Spanish–American War for the first time since the antebellum era. Rove's idea of a Republican majority was also based on a Southern strategy that stoked the politics of backlash against racial justice.

The Republican attempt to pursue the politics of national reconciliation at the expense of racial justice did not go unanswered, however. In a Memorial Day speech in 1878, the African American abolitionist and reformer Frederick Douglass reminded his audience that there 'was a right side and a wrong side in the late war'.

At the dawn of the twentieth century, W. E. B. Du Bois opened his meditation on race in the US, *The Souls of Black Folk*, by stating that 'the problem of the Twentieth Century is the problem of the color-line'.[55] Towards the end of the century, Du Bois's premonition still held true. The Republicans became the party of racial backlash after the Civil Rights era and ensured that the colour line would be a divisive issue even in the twenty-first century. Instead of the idea of *e pluribus unum* as the very definition of American identity that Obama had articulated in his speech to the Democratic Convention in 2004, the Republicans held on to the divisive racial politics of Nixonland.

In the first decades of the twentieth century, conservative narratives of American identity were couched in terms of purity and contamination exemplified by Anglo-Saxon roots as opposed to miscegenation. Thus the widespread fear of mongrelization, especially in the rapidly expanding metropolitan areas of the US, grew in the years of the second immigration wave from Southern and Eastern Europe. African American migration from South to North during these years did nothing to diminish the sense that the Anglo-Saxon centre would soon no longer hold.[56]

In 1915 *The Birth of a Nation*, D. W. Griffith's epic of the antebellum, the Civil War and Reconstruction eras, premiered in cinemas across the US. The timing of the film was poignant. It coincided with the fiftieth anniversary of the surrender of the South at a courthouse in Appomattox, Virginia. The film, however, was bent on turning military defeat into social and cultural victory. The onerous establishment of black rule in the South depicted in the film had turned the orderly Southern world upside down. It was payback time for the former slaves. Griffith offered scenes of whites out for a stroll on the sidewalks of the Southern towns forced to step aside for the new black rulers during the new social order of the Reconstruction era. Griffith's dark vision of a white supremacist world turned upside down has a long reach. In interviews conducted in York, Pennsylvania by National Public Radio in October, one respondent expressed the view that an Obama victory would mean 'payback time' for African Americans. She told the interviewers that

> I don't want to sound racist, and I'm not racist. But I feel if we put Obama in the White House, there will be chaos. I feel a lot of black people are going to feel it's payback time. And I made the statement, I said, 'You know, at one

time the black man had to step off the sidewalk when a white person came down the sidewalk.' And I feel it's going to be somewhat reversed. I really feel it's going to get somewhat nasty.[57]

In Griffith's narrative, however, the freed slaves, prodded by their nefarious Northern accomplices, are singularly unfit to rule. Lascivious and endemically lazy, the only legislation of note that the South Carolina legislature can muster up energy to pass is one permitting intermarriage between blacks and whites. To emphasize his point, Griffith has black legislators, their bulging eyes full of lust, ogle the flowers of Southern womanhood assembled in the galleries awaiting the outcome with trepidation. In the film's rousing climax, order is restored when the Ku Klux Klan ride to the rescue of the hapless female population.

This new Southern social order was not just a product of Griffith's imagination. The South may have lost the Civil War on the battlefield, but it won the peace. After the Reconstruction era, the former states of the Confederacy succeeded in stripping male African Americans of the right to vote guaranteed them by the Fourteenth Amendment to the Constitution. In 1896, the Supreme Court declared that separate facilities for blacks and whites was Constitutional. Michael Lind has, with some justification, called the period between the end of Reconstruction in 1876 and the 1970s the Confederate Century, a 'de facto Confederacy with the economy of a non-industrial resource colony, the social order of a racial caste society, and the politics of a one-party dictatorship'.[58]

The South remained an economic backwater for a good part of the twentieth century in some measure due to the stagnation of social and cultural life predicated by the separation of the races. The Southern model soon broke the confines of the region defined by the old Confederacy. In the 1970s, John Edgerton had identified what he called the Southernization of America. The year before, the first conservative Southerner since before the Civil War, Peter Applebome, observed that 'only the blind could look at America at the century's end and not see the fingerprint of the South on almost every aspect of the nation's soul'.[59]

For his part, McCain had no inhibitions about casting Obama in the role of both stranger and uppity black. Guided by the strategists who had worked for George W. Bush, some of whom had engaged in smearing McCain in his 2000 contest against Bush, and who were members in good standing of the Lee Atwater/Karl Rove school of the Republican attack machine, the McCain campaign proceeded to air ads characterizing the Republican candidate as 'the American president Americans have been waiting for' and Obama as a black man above his station, poised to prey on white women. In two ads that could be characterized as *Birth of a Nation* lite – 'Celeb' and 'Disrespectful' – the McCain campaign played on the timeworn theme of sexually charged blacks threatening white women. The ads were not without precedent. In 1988, George H. W. Bush's campaign manager Lee Atwater was responsible for one of the most nefarious ads in modern political history – the Willie Horton ad, which used the image of a paroled African American rapist to criticise the Democratic presidential candidate and current governor of Massachusetts Michael Dukakis's leniency on crime. In 2006, Republicans ran an ad against the Democratic candidate for Senate in Tennessee, Harold Ford, Jr, an African American, which featured a white woman, who claimed to have met Ford at a Playboy Club, winking at the camera and intoning, 'Call me, Harold.'[60]

The 'Celeb' ad was run in the wake of Obama's successful trip to the Middle East and Europe in the summer of 2008. It began by flashing images of Obama before adoring European crowds, accompanied by a voiceover declaring, 'He's the biggest celebrity in the world, but is he ready to lead?' The images from Berlin and the steady chants of the crowd conjured up memories of Nazi mass meetings. The implication was clear: Europeans and especially Germans were expressing the same herd mentality they had shown in the past and would follow a leader blindly. In the blink of an eye, two other images flashed across the screen – those of pop idols Britney Spears and Paris Hilton. The two young blonde celebrities functioned on several levels in the ad. Neither Spears nor Hilton is known for her intellectual acumen. As Democratic strategist Donna Brazile put it on the ABC programme *This Week*, they are, in a word, 'ditzes'. Something more sinister was also at work in the ad. *New York Times* columnist Bob Herbert observed that it was 'designed to exploit the hostility, anxiety and resentment of the many white Americans who are still freakishly hung up on the idea of black men rising above their station and becoming sexually involved with white women'.[61]

'Disrespectful' added to the impression of Obama as an African American who refused to stay in his place. Democratic vice-presidential candidate Joe Biden, known both for his verbosity and misstatements, had joked with a crowd at an Obama rally that the obvious difference between him and his opponent Sarah Palin was that she was 'good-looking'. The ad used the quote but placed it beside an image of Obama. It conveyed the impression that a black man was being disrespectful to a white woman.

In 1915, the same year as *The Birth of a Nation* pre-miered, the African American boxer Jack Johnson lost the Heavyweight Champion of the World title he had won in 1908 as the first African American to do so. Johnson enjoyed having himself photographed in the company of young white women, well aware that in the age of lynching such images would widely be regarded as a provocation. In 1955 a young African American boy from Chicago, Emmett Till, was brutally murdered in the small town of Money, Mississippi after he had allegedly whistled at a white woman at a convenience store. By the 1960s, however, the sight of interracial couples was in some circles no longer regarded as a provocation, even though interracial marriage was banned in seventeen states.

In 1967 the film *Guess Who's Coming to Dinner* tackled shifts in general attitudes towards interracial marriage head on. A white and very liberal San Francisco couple, Matt and Cristina Drayton, have their positive view of integration put to the test when their daughter Joey brings her fiancé home to meet her parents. The fiancé, Dr John Wade Prentice, is African American. When he is asked by Matt about what fate lies in store for their future children, Prentice cheerily replies that 'Joey feels that all of our children will be President of the United States'.

That same year, the Supreme Court decided to take on a case involving interracial marriage in Virginia. Three years before Obama's parents married, Richard Loving, a white man, and Mildred Jeter, a black woman, were arrested and jailed for violating Virginia state law. In other words, the union between Stanley Ann Dunham and Barack Hussein Obama, Sr would have been a crime in the state of Virginia and twenty-one other states. Arguing that the anti-miscegenation law violated the Due Process Clause and the Fourteenth Amendment to the Constitution, a unanimous Supreme Court declared it unconstitutional.

By the 1970s, an interracial couple – a white husband and African American wife – could be featured on the hit sitcom *The Jeffersons* that ran for ten seasons (1965–75). Since the 1967 Supreme Court ruling, the number of interracial marriages has increased exponentially in the United States. According to the Census Bureau, black–white marriages increased from 65,000 in 1970 to 422,000 in 2005. The ethnic intermarriage rate is even higher among US-born Latinos and Asians. Between a third and a half of these groups marry outside their ethnicity.

The Republican Party, which had employed racially coded rhetoric as part of its Southern strategy since 1968, was more than willing to conjure up memories of the rigid colour line of the past in an effect to cast Obama as an outsider. Obama, on the other hand, was the product of an interracial union of the kind that was becoming increasingly common and was likely to become even more widespread in the future. In this sense, Obama's complex identity anticipated trends taking hold in the late twentieth and early twenty-first centuries. The ineffectiveness of the ads was a measure not only of how out of touch the Republicans were, but of the extent to which the US had changed in the twenty years since the Willie Horton ad was aired.

As distasteful as they may have been, the ads 'Celeb' and 'Disrespectful' paled in comparison with the Jeremiah Wright controversy in the spring of 2008 that threatened to derail Obama's candidacy. Wright had been the head of Trinity United Church of Christ since 1972. Like a number of African American religious leaders, Wright had been influenced by the black liberation theology that grew out of the Civil Rights movement in the mid-60s. Jesus was often portrayed as a dark-skinned revolutionary in black liberation theology that had as its central text Jesus's words as recorded in chapter 4, verse 18 of the Gospel According to Luke:

> The Spirit of the Lord is upon me, because he hath anointed me to preach the gospel to the poor; he hath sent me to heal the brokenhearted, to preach deliverance to the captives, and recovering of sight to the blind, to set at liberty them that are bruised.

Wright's church was heavily engaged in social work in the South Side of Chicago. In his sermons, Wright had often blamed endemic racism in the US for the problems African Americans confronted.

From the McCain campaign to right-wing talk show and radio hosts like Bill O'Reilly and Rush Limbaugh, Wright's views were as roundly condemned as his association with Obama was emphasized. The clip of Wright shouting 'God damn America!' to his parishioners was played in a seemingly endless loop on TV and on the Internet.

As pressure mounted, Obama announced that he would give a major speech addressing the issue on 18 March in Philadelphia. The speech, 'A More Perfect Union', was remarkable not only because it used the Wright controversy to make a larger statement about race in the US. It also revealed how different Obama's vision of the US and American national identity was from the one that McCain and Palin were busy promoting on the campaign trail.

In his second book, *The Audacity of Hope*, Obama noted that there were commentators who had interpreted the line in his 2004 Convention speech, 'There is not a black America and a white America and Latino America and Asian America – there's the United States of America', to mean that the US had already achieved a post-racial politics and a colour-blind society. Obama sought to correct that impression by underscoring the salience of race while proposing ways to get beyond it. Thinking about race was like looking at a split screen, he argued, 'to maintain in our sights the kind of America that we want while looking squarely at America as it is, to acknowledge the sins of our past and the challenges of the present without becoming trapped in cynicism or despair'.[62]

Obama used two events in 2005 to illustrate his point. While attending the funeral of Rosa Parks, he reflected on how her single act of civil disobedience, refusing to give up her seat on a bus in Montgomery, Alabama to a white passenger, sparked the Civil Rights movement. In a ceremony infused with memories of the segregated South in 1955 and thoughts of the improvement in race relations in the half-century that followed, Obama could not help but think of another event that unfolded only two months previously. Hurricane Katrina had exposed the legacy of racial injustice and poverty that still plagued the US, but hope for 'a transformative moment . . . had quickly died away'. Honouring Rosa Parks's memory would necessitate more than the symbolic gestures of stamps and statues.[63]

Obama devoted much of the chapter on race in *The Audacity of Hope* to finding ways of bridging the racial divide by reconciling the political divide between conservative and liberal thought on race relations. He acknowledged that African Americans, as liberals believed, were burdened by the legacy of racism, but also, as conservatives argued, bore responsibility for improving their own condition. In 2004, comedian Bill Cosby had angered many in the African American community when he, speaking at an NAACP event to commemorate the fiftieth anniversary of the landmark Supreme Court decision on *Brown* v. *Board of Education*, launched into a rambling diatribe against parents who refused to take responsibility for their children and blamed crime and chronic black unemployment exclusively on systemic racism.[64] Later in the campaign, Obama would himself be criticised by the Reverend Jesse Jackson (in some off-colour comments made off-camera on the Fox network) for making similar remarks in a Father's Day speech. Unlike Cosby, however, Obama attempted to strike a balance between urging parental responsibility and recognizing the burdens of history.[65]

The same sentiments informed Obama's speech on race. In responding to the controversy over his personal relationship with Wright, Obama chose to place it in the larger context of the history of race relations in the US that went to the heart of American national identity. He acknowledged the gaps in understanding between white and black Americans while at the same time reminding his audience of the long struggle for racial justice. He used the idea of forming a more perfect union, enshrined in the first line of the US Constitution, to resolve the inherent contradiction between the 'stain' of slavery and the cause of freedom, both contained in the Constitution, in terms of a constant struggle over time.

According to Obama, the tension between current racial prejudices and the desire for racial reconciliation could be explained in these terms as well. As the son of a black Kenyan and a white Kansan who had chosen to be part of the African American community, Obama was in a unique position to understand the motivations behind the racial divide in the US from both sides. He spoke of black anger as well as white resentment in an attempt to come to grips with the flawed reasoning that sustained the gap between races. He acknowledged the legacy of slavery and racial injustice that still affected African Americans while arguing that blaming it alone would ultimately stifle any chance for change.

Indeed, what Obama characterised as Wright's 'profound mistake' was not that he spoke out against racism, but that 'he spoke as if our society was static; as if no progress has been made'. It was precisely this ahistorical way of looking at race that had led to a 'racial stalemate'. He linked the need to confront the issue of race with his own message for change and called for an end to the politics of cynicism (perhaps an implicit jab at the race-baiting of the Republicans) and the need to address the problems that confronted all Americans, regardless of race or ethnic background.[66]

The speech was not only an appeal to Americans to live up to the creed of *e pluribus unum* but also an attempt to see the promise of the US not as a static set of ideals, but as a continuing effort towards creating a more perfect union.

As a member of a new generation of black politicians with no personal memory of the Civil Rights movement, Obama has had to overcome the skepticism that many of the older generation of leaders voiced about the viability of his candidacy. Two veterans of the Civil Rights movement, James Clyburn, the House Majority Whip (D-SC), and John Lewis, a Democratic Congressman from Georgia, initially held back in endorsing Obama. As Matt Bai put it in a long essay about the rise of a new generation of African American politicians,

> For a lot of younger African Americans, the resistance of the Civil Rights generation to Obama's candidacy signified the failure of their parents to come to terms, at the dusk of their lives, with the success of their own struggle – to embrace the idea that black politics might now be disappearing into American politics in the same way that the Irish and Italian machines long ago joined the political mainstream.[67]

Less than a month after he announced that he would run for president, Obama attempted to persuade the older generation of African Americans of the viability of his candidacy. In a speech at Brown Chapel AME Church commemorating the Voting Rights march in Selma, Obama paid tribute to the Civil Rights generation:

> I'm here because somebody marched. I'm here because you all sacrificed for me. I stand on the shoulders of giants. I thank the Moses generation; but we've got to remember, now, that Joshua still had a job to do.[68]

Quoting Robert F. Kennedy, who observed that the Civil Rights movement sent 'ripples of hope all around the world', he deftly interwove his father's desire to come to the US with the message of racial justice. Looking to the future, he talked at length about the unfinished business the Joshua generation needed to accomplish.

Obama will likely, as a national politician, confront the same dilemmas that other young leaders like Deval Patrick and Cory Booker are dealing with at the state and local level. A Pew Research Center survey published at the end of 2007 found a values gap between middle-class and poor blacks as well as a general attitude of pessimism about the state of black progress.[69] Many young black leaders come from the growing black middle class and are highly educated. As state and local leaders, however, they confront cities and districts with high rates of black poverty. Unlike the Civil Rights era, no legal barriers exist to prevent black progress. Yet inequities between black and white society persist. The new generation of black politicians is clearly aware of these disparities but must walk a fine line in order not to be perceived as favouring the African American community. Furthermore, while a President Barack Obama will clearly serve as a role model to young blacks, his success can erode the already fragile support for affirmative action programmes. Paradoxically, the first African American president may well find it difficult to fight against racial injustice or champion programmes to help improve the plight of the urban poor.

Despite these possible problems, Obama is unwavering in his belief that transformative change is not only possible, but necessary. In his victory speech in Grant Park, Chicago on 4 November, Obama offered a poignant example of how the arc of history is bent towards justice. He told the story of Ann Nixon Cooper, who at 106 years old was born the year after Booker T. Washington became the first African American to attend a formal dinner at the White House, and the year before W. E. B. Du Bois penned his prophetic words in *The Souls of Black Folk*. Cooper, Obama reminded the jubilant crowd that had gathered to celebrate his election as the forty-fourth president of the United States:

> was born just a generation past slavery; a time when there were no cars on the road or planes in the sky; when someone like her couldn't vote for two reasons – because she was a woman and because of the color of her skin.[70]

Obama cited a litany of the momentous transformations during the twentieth century brought about by war, social movements and science to drive home his point that the US is not, as Wright would have it, irrevocably racist and the American people not forever susceptible to coded racism, as the Republicans might like to think. Ann Nixon Cooper's freedom to vote is part of a larger story of the meaning of freedom. If freedom is central to American national identity, the story of Ann Nixon Cooper is testimony to the fact that freedom is not a fixed category but has been subject to changing definitions as a result of debates and struggles.

In *The Audacity of Hope*, Obama made it clear that he does not regard his own identity as bound by race. His own biracial background and upbringing in polyglot Hawaii and Muslim Indonesia has contributed to his belief that the US has the 'ability to absorb newcomers, to forge a national identity out of the disparate lot that arrived on our shores'.[71] He does not see an inherent contradiction in the absorption of immigrants and his characterization of the US as a multicultural nation. In this sense, he adheres to what historian Gordon Wood has called a 'soft' multiculturalism that recognises the compatibility of cultural diversity and national pride.[72]

Competing narratives

The competing narratives of Obama in the 2008 election cycle thus have deep roots in the ongoing debate over American national identity. 'Who is Barack Obama?,' the Republicans asked and then proceeded to answer with pointed barbs about past associations and spurious claims that Obama was somehow less than 100 per cent American. Obama represented the obverse of the Republican narrative of national identity. Obama's two books and the life story he and his surrogates presented during the course of his presidential campaign form a counternarrative of what it means to be an American in the twenty-first century. The Republican narrative is static and bound to the past. Obama's counternarrative is fluid, as he stated in the 2004 preface to *Dreams from My Father*, and in many respects conforms to the emerging national identity of the twenty-first century.

Obama has often referred to his background as unusual and his quest in national politics as improbable. His background, however, is only unique in the sense that it embodies so many aspects of American national identity at so many junctures of US history. Obama may well be the first African American president, but he shares Irish roots with a number of other recent presidents – including Kennedy, Reagan and Clinton. His mother, Stanley Ann Dunham, was of Irish heritage. In 1850, one of his mother's ancestors, Fulmouth Kearny, emigrated from Ireland to the US. Little record remains of his life, but it is not unreasonable to speculate that Obama's maternal ancestors may have suffered from the widespread prejudices prevailing against Irish immigrants at the time.

Ironically, it was the campaign of the wife of the descendent of Irish immigrants and the man Toni Morrison once called the 'first black president' that provided the Republicans with inspiration for their playbook on Obama's less-than-American identity. Mark Penn, Hillary Rodham Clinton's chief strategist, had achieved a modicum of fame in the 1996 election between Bill Clinton and Bob Dole for coining the epithet 'soccer mom' to describe middle-class suburban women who spend time transporting their children to various extra-curricular activities after school. A Canadian variation of this term, 'hockey mom', was used by Sarah Palin in the 2008 campaign. In his book *Microtrends*, Penn went against the very notion of the One America theme that Obama struck in his 2004 Convention speech and that became a hallmark of his 2008 campaign:

This book is all about the niching of America. How there is no One America anymore, or Two, or Three, or Eight. In fact, there are hundreds of Americas, hundreds of new niches made up of people drawn together by common interests.[73]

Penn was determined to stamp Obama as a kind of micro-trend unto his own, representing only a negligible fraction of the American people. In March 2007, he fired off a memo to Hillary Clinton that laid out a possible strategy for her in her primary campaign against Obama:

All of these articles about his boyhood in Indonesia and his life in Hawaii are geared towards showing his background is diverse, multicultural and putting that in a new light.
Save it for 2050.
It also exposes a very strong weakness for him – his roots to basic American values and culture are at best limited. I cannot imagine America electing a president during a time of war who is not at his center fundamentally American in his thinking and in his values.[74]

It has been said that Hillary Clinton chose to ignore Penn's sage advice. This is only partially true. While Clinton did not overtly brand Obama for his supposed 'lack of American roots', she did what she could to underscore her own. She expressed concern about Obama's weak support among 'hard-working Americans, white Americans' who were voting for her in the primaries. It didn't help matters when Obama, speaking at a San Francisco fundraiser in February, explained the consequences of job loss in small towns in Pennsylvania and the Midwest by saying that 'it's not surprising then that they get bitter, they cling to guns or religion or antipathy to people who aren't like them or anti-immigrant sentiment or anti-trade sentiment as a way to explain their frustrations'. What came to be known as Bittergate cast Obama as an elitist, out of touch with the experiences of ordinary Americans.[75]

For good measure, husband Bill played the patriotic card, proclaiming on the campaign trail in North Carolina in March that with Hillary Clinton and John McCain, Americans would have a choice between 'two people who love this country'. Particularly in primaries in the Appalachian region, Clinton pursued a strategy of divisiveness similar to that of the McCain/Palin campaign.

The McCain/Palin strategy of casting Obama as the ultimate stranger was doomed to fail because the real America was simply no longer what McCain and Palin thought it to be. Their message ended up appealing to an ever-shrinking base. The disconnect between what most Americans saw as their national identity and the anachronistic identity put forward by the Republicans proved to be the undoing of the McCain/Palin campaign. This is by no means to suggest that identity was the sole reason for the defeat of the Republican ticket in 2008. That it played a crucial role, however, is beyond question. In this sense, the election of 2008 was the first election of the twenty-first century in which white Americans will no longer be the majority.

The two conventions themselves, however, were a study in contrasts. A glance at their delegates underscores the difference between the old America of the Republicans and the emerging America of the Democrats. The delegates to the Republican National Convention in St Paul were 93 per cent white, only 5 per cent Latino and a mere 1.5 per cent African American. At the Democratic National Convention in Denver, a full 34 per cent of the delegates were either African American or Latino.[76]

By mid-century, minorities will be the majority in the US, according to the Census Bureau. Even now, white non-Hispanics are only 66 per cent of the population. A full 45 per cent of Americans under five years old are non-white.

The change can be measured by looking to the past. In 1972, minorities were a mere 10 per cent of the electorate. By 2008, their percentage of the electorate had more than doubled, to 26 per cent. The white working class, which was 58 per cent of the workforce in 1940, had diminished to 25 per cent in 2006.[77]

Somos americanos

Two narratives – one an attempt to hold onto Nixonland, one cosmopolitan and transnational – became part of the quadrennial plebescite on the future of US national identity. Both have deep roots in the American past. Both envision an entirely different future for the United States. One side proposes rigid and impermeable borders, both mental and physical, while the other side acknowledges the fluidity of identity that Obama spoke of in his autobiography and celebrates the diversity that Obama praised in his inaugural address.

In 2006, the national anthem was translated into Spanish and released as 'Nuestro Himno'. That same year, demonstrations were organized under the slogan 'A Day Without Immigrants', to emphasize the vital role immigrants, both documented and undocumented, play in the American economy. Many demonstrators carried banners reading 'Somos americanos' – proclaiming their belonging to the US, in Spanish. The transnationalist and cosmopolitan narrative, which could, in light of the demonstrations of 2006, be called the narrative of 'somos americanos', tells another story of the future of the United States. The very utterance 'somos americanos' goes against the grain of this exclusionist view. It recognizes that immigrants can maintain dual allegiances and still be regarded as belonging to American society. The failed presidential candidate Tom Tancredo sees the meaning of citizenship in narrow terms. He thus calls for an end to birthright citizenship for illegal aliens and the elimination

Identities

of dual citizenship.[78] Similarly, Samuel Huntington rails against 'the rise of powerful political forces promoting dual loyalties, dual identities, and dual citizenship'.[79]

'Somos americanos', on the other hand, accepts dual identities as a reflection of the transnational dimension of current immigration. The transnational or cosmopolitan narrative recognizes the impurity of all cultures, as Anthony Kwame Appiah so vividly describes it in *Cosmopolitanism*.[80] In *Identity and Violence*, Sen argues against the reductionism of civilizationist thinking and makes a case for looking at the plurality of affiliations that constitute identity.[81] The new immigrants from the rest of Latin America, the Caribbean, the Middle East, Africa and Asia are contributing to the cultural contamination that Appiah sees as the true meaning of cosmopolitanism. No wall or fence, however sophisticated, can stop this cosmopolitan future.

Conservatives like Huntington fear that current immigration rates will lead to the Balkanization of the United States. Obama expresses no such fear. In discussing the 'demographic realities of America's future' he merely states that the prospect of the US becoming a majority–minority nation by the year 2050 will likely bring unanticipated consequences.

Obama is at odds with those conservative commentators and Republican Party politicians who regard the idea of fluid identity as suspect and who have constructed a narrow nationalism based on nostalgia for small-town America to appease their ever-shrinking electoral base. In the war over American national identity, the Republican strategy of casting Obama as a stranger with a lack of American roots ignored precisely not only the profound social, economic and demographic changes that have taken place since the mid-1960s, but the transformation in attitudes towards race and immigration that followed in their wake. It was these factors that in the end helped propel Obama to the White House.

An American for the twenty-first century

In her perceptive essay, 'What it Means to be an American in the 21st Century', Tamar Jacoby calls for the articulation of a new narrative that draws on past conceptions of national identity but also adapts to the realities of a twenty-first-century world marked by globalization, the integration of international labour markets, and the ease and availability of international travel and communications. She calls for a 'tempered multiculturalism' that acknowledges difference within a shared identity. A minimalist identity of adherence to American ideals is not sufficient. Like Obama's ideal of bending the arc of history, Jacoby seeks to 'highlight the long, hard struggle that has been the forging of our national identity'.[82]

It would perhaps be to indulge in hyperbole to claim that Obama is a representative man for the twenty-first century. Nevertheless, Obama's identities, which he imagined gave his candidacy an 'unlikely' tincture and which the McCain/Palin campaign insisted on characterizing as having only a tenuous connection to the US, are ultimately more representative of 'who we are' in the twenty-first century than the retrograde, narrow vision proffered by the GOP. The election of 2008 pitted the transformations brought about by the Civil Rights movements and the identity movements that followed in their wake, as well as the transnational nature of the new immigration and the effects of internal migration, against an outworn Southern strategy and outmoded appeals to nativism. The outcome of the election may not have ended the culture wars over American national identity but it may, with time, be regarded as a turning point in favour of those who, with Obama, see the US as a multicultural nation.

The Republican attempt to make Nixonland a permanent condition of the American national character ended with a pale imitation – Palinland. McCain was marginal to this project. In one of the many ironies of American political history, the term Nixonland was coined in 1956 by Adlai Stevenson's speechwriter, the economist John Kenneth Galbraith. Not only is Galbraith's notion of 'countervailing institutions,' i.e. a robust public sphere to offset the excesses of an unregulated private sector, back in fashion in the wake of the financial crisis; Galbraith saw Nixonland as a dire threat to American society. He was prompted to focus on Vice President Nixon because of a number of health scares President Eisenhower suffered in the months leading up to the election of 1956.[83] The prospect of a President Nixon in 1956 was too much for Galbraith to bear. In 2008, the prospect of a President Palin was all too real, given that McCain, who would have been the oldest president ever elected, had a history of health issues.

The politics of resentment and racial backlash have for forty years dominated American politics and have shaped notions of the American national character. Those within the Republican Party who would continue the culture wars along the battle lines of the Southern strategy and neonativism will consign their party to minority status for the foreseeable future. Obama's candidacy and election, by highlighting the successes of the Civil Rights movement and the changing face of immigration, can contribute to the articulation of a new narrative for American national identity in the twenty-first century.

2
Grassroots

Grassroots victory

When Barack Obama stood on the steps of the old Capitol Building in Springfield, Illinois on 10 February 2007 to announce that he would seek his party's nomination for president of the United States, he started by telling his audience how he came to Chicago in 1985. He was offered a low-paying job as a community organizer and ended up working in some of the poorest neighbourhoods in the city, where he 'received the best education I ever had'.[84]

When Obama spoke at Grant Park on 4 November 2008 shortly after the networks announced that he had won the presidential election, he made a point of thanking his organizers in the field. He emphasized that his campaign was at heart a grassroots effort, begun 'in the backyards of Des Moines and the living rooms of Concord and the front porches of Charleston' and funded primarily by small donors. Evoking Lincoln, as he had done so many times during his campaign, Obama paid tribute to the millions of Americans who volunteered, and organized, and proved that more than two centuries later a 'government of the people, by the people and for the people has not perished from the Earth'. The election did not end the importance of volunteerism and grassroots organizing. Obama extended the spirit of community organizing to the challenges facing the nation by calling for a 'new spirit of service, a new spirit of sacrifice'.[85]

To underscore the importance of continuing the grassroots work that had been so vital to his victory, the campaign organization, Obama for America, changed its name to Organizing for America days after Obama was inaugurated.

The Promised Land

In *Dreams from My Father*, Obama highlighted the significance of Chicago and community organizing for his future development as a politician. Indeed the longest section of the book is devoted to his career as a community organizer.

Obama came to Chicago by chance. After graduating from high school in Hawaii, he moved to the mainland in 1979 and attended Occidental College. He transferred to Columbia College in New York City and graduated in 1983 with a major in political science. That same year, according to his autobiography, he 'decided to become a community organizer'.[86] By his own admission, his conception of what a community organizer did was vague at best. When pressed by friends to define community organizing, Obama resorted to speaking of it as a vehicle for change in the US.

Change won't come from the top, I would say. Change will come from a mobilized grass roots.[87]

In contrast with Chicago, Obama chose not to discuss his years in New York City in great detail in his autobiography.[88] Even though he may have decided on a career in community organizing in 1983, after he graduated from Columbia College he worked for the Business International Corporation, a research firm that helped companies planning operations abroad understand overseas markets (it was bought by the Economist Intelligence Unit in 1986). It was only in 1984 that Obama was hired by the New York Public Interest Research Group (NYPIRG), a consumer, environmental and government reform organization. According to Obama, his motivation for getting involved in community organizing was twofold. He was inspired by the Civil Rights movement, which he referred to as a 'past I had never known'. He believed that membership in the community, be it the African American or the larger American community, could be earned through organizing. Through organizing, someone with his unique and itinerant background could find a place to belong.[89] According to his co-workers at the NYPIRG, Obama worked on a campaign to improve the City College of New York subway station and on the divestment campaign against South Africa at the City University of New York, and led voter registration drives.[90] In his autobiography, however, Obama gives the impression that the results of his organizing in New York was limited and the work itself frustrating. In search of inspiration, he went to Columbia to attend a talk by Kwame Ture, who as Stokely Carmichael was one of the leaders of the Student Non-Violating Coordinating Committee and was credited with coining the phrase Black Power. When a woman in the audience questioned the feasibility of Ture's idea of establishing direct economic links between Harlem and Africa, she was criticized for her bourgeois attitudes. Obama left the meeting clearly disillusioned with the fragmentation of what had once been a united Civil Rights movement and unsure of his future as a community organizer.[91]

It was at this low point that Obama received a call from a community organizer in Chicago, whom he elected to call Marty Kaufman, but who is likely Gerald Kellman.[92] Kellman persuaded Obama to come to Chicago to work for the Developing Communities Project (DCP), a new organization that grew out of a community group based in churches in the inner city. The community group was working in white, Latino and African American areas affected by the rash of steel mill closings. The DCP would target African American neighbourhoods.

In spite of the meagre salary – only $10,000 a year – Obama accepted the job and moved to Chicago in 1985. Apart from his three years at Harvard Law School (1988–91), Obama has lived in Chicago ever since – for nearly a quarter of a century. The previously itinerant Obama found a home and community there. In this sense, he can be called a 'rooted cosmopolitan'. Chicago shaped his identity as well as his politics. He bonded with the African American community and his experience of community organizing would influence the way that he perceived politics not as top-down management but as a bottom-up endeavour based on volunteerism.

Chicago has a rich history of social work, labour agitation and African American politics. The black population of Chicago was at the end of the nineteenth century a paltry 2 per cent. That changed during the first decades of the twentieth century. The deteriorating state of race relations in the South in the post-Reconstruction era, along with the social and legal segregation instituted in the former states of the Confederacy and accepted by the federal government and the Supreme Court in the name of national reconciliation, coupled with hard times for the backward economy, prompted many African Americans to seek their fortune in the rapidly industrializing Northern states. In the first decades of the twentieth century, African Americans migrated north in large numbers. During what came to be called the Great Migration from 1916 to 1970, around 7 million African Americans left the Jim Crow South for the promised land of the North. Half a million came to Chicago alone. By 1970, the black population of Chicago was at 33 per cent. It currently has the second largest African American population (after New York City) in the US.[93]

Even though the manufacturing sector of Chicago grew precipitously in the first decades of the twentieth century, African Americans had to compete with the growing immigrant population for jobs. Ethnic and racial tension often gave rise to social unrest. One of the worst riots occurred just after the end of World War I. From 27 July to 3 August 1919, the South Side of Chicago witnessed violence and arson that left fifteen whites and twenty-three blacks dead. The Jamaican American poet Claude McKay wrote 'If We Must Die' in response to the riot. The poem, with its defiant last lines – 'Like men we'll face the murderous, cowardly pack,/Pressed to the wall, dying, but fighting back!' – became a symbol for black resistance in the face of oppression.[94] Although the ostensible reason for the riot was the drowning of an African American teenager who had crossed the invisible line separating white and black beaches, the underlying cause was competition over jobs, especially white resentment of employers using African Americans as strikebreakers.

Organizing for Chicago

African Americans were disproportionately affected by the onset of the Great Depression at the end of the 1920s. By 1932, the year Franklin D. Roosevelt was elected president, almost half of African American workers in the city of Chicago were unemployed. African Americans did benefit from New Deal largesse, however. As part of the Public Works Administration, a housing development named after Ida B. Wells was built in 1941, the largest of its kind.

After World War II, another housing project on the South Side, the Altgeld Gardens, was built to accommodate returning African American war veterans. It was here, in the 1980s, that Obama was sent to help residents secure grants for a jobs programme and work for asbsetos removal.

Obama came to Chicago during a period of transition.

When Martin Luther King, Jr decided to bring his campaign for racial justice to the North in 1965, he encountered unexpected resistance in Chicago, which was known for carving out racially segregated districts by redlining. Chicago radicalized King, causing him to advocate fundamental institutional changes to promote economic equality. One of King's closest associates, Jesse Jackson, set up Operation Breadbasket to pressure businesses to hire African Americans and to create black-controlled financial institutions. African American political and economic power grew in subsequent years and in 1983, two years before Obama arrived, Harold Washington was elected the first African American mayor of Chicago.[95] Washington had the misfortune of governing Chicago in the era of Reagan's New Federalism, which drastically cut direct aid to cities.[96] Obama could experience first-hand the consequences of the Reagan administration's starving of urban areas.

In Chicago, Obama encountered not only the effects of the African American migration that had produced large inner-city communities and the sometimes bitter legacy of racial politics in the city. He was also exposed to the community organizing that was part of a long tradition of social work in the city.

Obama was quickly introduced to the strategy for community organizing developed by Saul Alinsky. Alinsky was something of a legend in Chicago. In 1906, the novelist Upton Sinclair had portrayed in *The Jungle* the poverty and horrendous working conditions in the meatpacking plants in the Back of the Yards district of Chicago. Alinsky formed the The Back of the Yards Neighborhood Council (BYNC) in 1939. The BYNC became a model for the kind of community organizing that Alinsky advocated to improve social conditions. This tradition for social work in Chicago goes back to the beginning of the Progressive era with the settlement house movement started by Jane Addams.[97]

Sinclair's vivid description of the Back of the Yards

district focused on the lives of Lithuanian immigrants working under horrendous conditions in the meatpacking plants and his muckraking novel had an impact beyond its wide readership. Meat sales dropped by half and there was a public outcry against the lack of oversight in the meatpacking industry. As a direct result of Sinclair's exposure of substandard and unhygienic working conditions, Congress passed the Meat Inspection Act and the Pure Food and Drug Act which effectively created the Food and Drug Administration.

In an article written in 1988, three years after he came to Chicago, Obama offered an effective brief for the value of community organizing. He saw community organizing as a vital part of political empowerment for African Americans at a time when black inner-city communities were suffering from economic cutbacks imposed by the Reagan administration. He recognized the problems facing black political leaders like Harold Washington in trying to govern with limited resources. While Obama applauded the 'surge of political empowerment' that grew out of the Civil Rights movement and which in Chicago resulted in the election of Washington, and while Obama welcomed economic development strategies promoted by local entrepreneurs, they alone could not solve the problems facing inner-city communities:

> In my view, however, neither approach offers lasting hope of real change for the inner city unless undergirded by a systematic approach to community organization.[98]

Although he does not mention Saul Alinsky, Obama certainly had him in mind when he wrote that Chicago 'was the birthplace of community organizing'.[99] His article attests to the influence Alinsky had on his thinking. He clearly agrees with Alinsky's dictum that it is necessary to deal with 'the world as it is, not our wished-for fantasy of the world as it should be'.[100] Alinsky regarded communication as the most important element of organizing. As he put it, 'Since people understand only in terms of their own experience, an organizer must have at least a cursory familiarity with their experience.'[101] Obama's campaign organization would emphasize the importance of listening to people's stories in order to establish deep communication with potential voters.

In his article on organizing, Obama argued that, in the face of underfunded city governments and middle-class flight from the inner city, an absolutely vital factor was 'harnessing the internal productive capacities' of inner-city residents. He went on to list some of the achievements of his own organization, the Developing Communities Project, and other organizations in Chicago.

Schools have been made more accountable; job training programs have been established; housing has been renovated and built; city services have been provided; parks have been refurbished; and crime and drug problems have been curtailed. Additionally, plain folk have been able to access the levers of power, and a sophisticated pool of local civic leadership has been developed.[102]

Writing only a decade after Obama came to Chicago, sociologist William Julius Wilson offered a sober assessment of the plight of the urban poor in the opening line of his book *When Work Disappears*: 'For the first time in the twentieth century most adults in many inner-city neighborhoods are not working in a typical week'.[103]

As Wilson observed, the passage of the Housing Act in 1949 established lower-income ceilings for residency in public housing that led to the concentration of the most disadvantaged groups in the new housing projects. Resistance from middle- and working-class whites forced the Federal Public Housing Authority to build low-cost housing in inner-city ghettos. The New Federalism of the Reagan administration had meant sharp cuts in direct spending to cities that had exacerbated problems of employment and social cohesion in already depressed areas.[104]

The voice of one teenager growing up in the Ida B. Wells housing project in the 1980s and 1990s expressed the effect that the physical isolation and lack of opportunity had on the residents: 'We live in two different Americas. In the ghetto, our laws are totally different, our language is totally different, and our lives are totally different. I've never felt American. I've only felt African American.'[105] An elderly resident offered a simple explanation for the desperate situation of the Ida B. Wells: 'The main thing is no jobs.'[106]

Obama entered this other America when he came to Altgeld Gardens. It presented a unique challenge to the new community organizer. In *Dreams*, he describes the bleak landscape of the housing project. Located close to a sewage treatment plant, the original vision of decent low-cost housing for the African American poor had been destroyed by cynical political considerations that segregated Altgeld Gardens from white neighbourhoods.

Working with the residents of Altgeld Gardens proved transformative for Obama. He arranged for a number of residents to ride with him by bus to the local housing authority to persuade them to remove asbestos from the housing project: 'I changed as a result of that bus trip, in a fundamental way . . . That bus ride kept me going, I think. Maybe it still does.'[107]

There were the inevitable frustrations and setbacks. Obama recounts a meeting that Jerry Kellman (called Marty in *Dreams*) had arranged with union officials from the local LTV Steel plant and Angela, a resident from Altgeld. The meeting went badly. The union officials, who were being pressured by management for wage concessions, greeted Kellman's proposals for a worker buyout of the plant unenthusiastically. What was worse, in Obama's view, was Angela's reaction. She doubted the relevance of a few union jobs in an area suffering from chronic unemployment. Marty's miscalculation was his desire to forget the past. African Americans like Angela couldn't forget the past injustices levelled against her grandparents, who couldn't join a union, or her parents, who didn't have access to patronage jobs. Obama explained that 'for someone like Angela, the past *was* the present; it determined her world with a force infinitely more real than any notions of class solidarity. It explained why more blacks hadn't been able to move out into the suburbs while the going was still good, why more blacks hadn't climbed up the ladder to the American dream . . . It explained Altgeld.'[108] Obama's sensitivity to the burdens of past injustices would later inform his campaign rhetoric.

Obama did make a difference. His efforts helped some residents obtain employment and a number of apartments at Altgeld were cleared of asbestos. However, in spite of these successes, it was perhaps Angela's recognition that incremental improvements were insufficient in effecting lasting change that prompted Obama to apply to law school.

Obama's successor, Johnnie Owens, recalled that Obama was consciously seeking a larger role for himself. As Owens put it, 'I do remember him saying at that time that the country was politically in a more conservative mode but that things operated in cycles and that a much more liberal mindset would begin to develop in the country and he wanted to be prepared to be an effective leader.'[109]

The power of the vote

Obama left Chicago to attend Harvard Law School in 1988. In 1990 he became the first African American to be elected president of the prestigious *Harvard Law Review*. Upon his return to Chicago, he joined a law firm as well as the local chapter of Project Vote, another grassroots organization dedicated to registering low-income and minority groups to vote. No doubt Obama's admiration for the struggles of the Civil Rights movement prompted him to join an organization like this. Between 1890 and 1906, every state in the former Confederacy passed laws restricting the African American vote. Intimidation and poll tax and grandfather clause provisions succeeded in depressing voting among African Americans in the South. In the postwar era, however, the NAACP launched a voter registration drive in the South that resulted in nearly 20 per cent of African Americans being registered to vote. In the summer of 1961, the year Obama was born, the Student Non-violent Coordinating Committee (SNCC) decided to send 'field secretaries' to the South, to engage in grassroots organizing to get African Americans to register to vote. The culmination of the voter registration drives by Civil Rights organizations came at the beginning of 1965 when Martin Luther King, Jr launched a campaign in Selma, Alabama. When King tried to bring the campaign from Selma to Montgomery, marchers were assaulted by state police. One of the marchers who was beaten by the police was John Lewis; he is currently a Democratic Congressman from Georgia and became an Obama supporter after first endorsing Hillary Clinton.

These grassroots efforts led to the passage of the 1965 Voting Rights Act that outlawed the discriminatory practices instituted by the southern states. In urging Congress to pass the legislation, President Lyndon B. Johnson quoted the old Civil Rights anthem, 'We Shall Overcome'. Johnson was well aware of the political consequences of his unwavering support for Civil Rights. In signing another piece of landmark legislation, the Civil Rights Act of 1964, LBJ said to Bill Moyers, his Press Secretary, 'I think we just delivered the South to the Republican party for a long time to come.'[110] LBJ's words were prophetic. In 2008 Barack Obama would be the first Democratic presidential candidate to win the southern state of Virginia since 1964.

In 1992, Democratic presidential candidate Bill Clinton hoped to win Illinois, which in 1988 Michael Dukakis had lost to George H. W. Bush by only a slim margin. The Democratic Party in Illinois had nominated Carol Moseley Braun as its candidate for Senate. If she won the election, she would become the first African American woman in the Senate. For the 1992 campaign, Obama launched Project Vote's media campaign with the slogan, 'It's a Power Thing' and recruited volunteers from community organizations and African American churches. Obama and his team managed to register more than 150,000 voters in six months. Clinton won Illinois and Moseley Braun won her seat in the Senate. A report published in *Chicago Magazine* in 1993 concluded that the increase in turnout had been crucial to the Democratic victory.[111] Through his work at Project Vote Obama also forged connections with Chicago's African American leadership that would prove invaluable to his later political career.

3
Networks

It's the networks, stupid

During his campaign for the presidency, Obama spoke often and glowingly of what his work as a community organizer meant to him. At one point during the autumn, the McCain/Palin campaign decided to use his past against him. Palin compared her job as the former mayor of Wasilla with Obama's community organizing, saying facetiously that while her job could also be regarded as a form of community organizing, the difference was that it involved real responsibility. Obama would, however, draw on his experience as a community organizer not only for the presidential campaign, but as a tool for governing.

Obama's presidential campaign operated on a fusion of the old-fashioned tactics of community organizing he learned in Chicago and the conscious updating of the netroots campaign that had, for a time, propelled Howard Dean to frontrunner status in the 2004 Democratic presidential campaign. It proved to be a powerful combination and was a crucial element in Obama's victory over Hillary Clinton in the primaries.

One of the strengths of the Obama campaign was its appeal to younger voters. In 2004, many young voters flocked to Howard Dean's campaign and ended up supporting Kerry. The swift-boating of John Kerry in the 2004 campaign, i.e. casting doubts about Kerry's heroism as a commander of a Swift Boat unit during the Vietnam War, did not resonate with younger voters, who knew little and cared less about the conflicts that preoccupied Baby Boomers. In *The Audacity of Hope*, Obama revealed his impatience with the endless bickering of the generation that preceded his.

> In the back-and-forth between Clinton and Gingrich, and in the elections of 2000 and 2004, I sometimes felt as if I were watching the psychodrama of the baby boom generation – a tale rooted in old grudges and revenge plots hatched on a handful of college campuses long ago – played out on the national stage.[112]

Obama's negative opinion of the Baby Boomer generation neglected the degree to which he, and indeed many of his age group, were indebted to it. The Baby Boom generation is usually defined as those Americans born between the end of World War II and the early 1960s. It has often been unfavourably compared to the generation preceding it, the so-called Greatest Generation. However, Obama and his generation as well as subsequent generations have been inspired by various movements that were either created or revived by the Baby Boom generation, including the environmental movement, the women's movement and of course the Civil Rights movement.[113] Many of his most ardent supporters came from yet another generation, often called Millennials, born between 1982 and 2003. Millennials voted overwhelmingly for Obama. According to Michael D. Hais and Morley Winograd, this generation will have a profound impact on elections to come, creating 'a new landscape of collective purpose and national consensus that involves individuals and communities in solving the nation's problems'.[114]

The Obama campaign also took a page from Bush strategist Karl Rove's playbook. After Bush lost the popular vote to Al Gore in the election of 2000, in part because of organized labour's efforts on behalf of the Democratic candidate, Rove set about improving the GOP strategy for 2004. He built an organization that recruited local volunteers, particularly in exurban and rural areas, who could bring Bush's message to their neighbours. He developed micro-targeting techniques designed to identify independents and Republicans, who could be persuaded to vote for Bush.[115]

This strategy proved to be particularly effective in the key state of Ohio, which Kerry lost by about 120,000 votes. Had Kerry won just over 60,000 more votes in Ohio, he would have become president. Rove instigated a massive get-out-the-vote campaign among evangelical Christians and gun-rights supporters in the conservative, southwestern part of the state that put his candidate over the top.

The difference between Rove's campaign and the one mounted by Obama in 2008 lay of course in the constituencies to which they were appealing. Rove targeted the Republican base, while the Obama campaign was busy forging a new Democratic coalition for the twenty-first century.

In running for president, Obama was determined to bring the lessons he had learned as a community organizer in Chicago to the spirit as well as the mechanics of his campaign. He set about creating a campaign from the bottom up that called upon Americans to revive the time-honoured tradition of community service and combined old-fashioned volunteerism with the newest technologies.

Obama learned two things from Howard Dean – how to use online technology to reach potential supporters and the importance of conducting a fifty-state strategy. Shortly after he was elected as the new chairman of the Democratic National Committee in February 2005, Howard Dean, the former governor of Vermont who for a time in 2004 was the frontrunner for the Democratic presidential nomination, announced that he would pursue a fifty-state strategy in planning for the 2008 election cycle. No state would be off limits. The Democratic Party would establish a visible presence in every state in order to work towards breaking the pattern of the elections of 2000 and 2004 with Republicans winning in the South and West and the Democrats confined to the two coasts and upper Midwest by making the Democrats competitive in a larger number of states.

Dean's fifty-state strategy met with widespread ridicule. What was the point, critics asked, of spending a lot of time and money setting up operations in reliably red states like Mississippi and Wyoming? Better to concentrate efforts in swing states like Ohio than to squander them in a futile attempt to colour the entire country purple.

Hillary Clinton paid lip service to Dean's fifty-state strategy, but her small inner circle of strategists devised an old-style campaign that relied on big donors with little outreach to grassroots organizations.[116] Mark Penn, Clinton's top adviser, drawing on the interpretation he had set forth in his book *Microtrends*, seemed more interested in targeting specific groups than in expanding the party's base.

For Barack Obama, however, the Dean strategy had its appeal for several reasons. First, it would underscore his message of bringing the country together instead of dividing it into red and blue segments. Second, the Obama campaign was attempting a voter registration drive reminiscent of the one that Obama had headed in Chicago for Project Vote in 1992. By setting up field operations in as many states as possible, Obama could mobilize groups that had not previously taken part in the political process. Furthermore, the idea of reaching out to marginalized groups would conform to Obama's message of conducting politics from the bottom up.

By Super Tuesday, the Obama campaign had set up field offices in all twenty-four states that were voting in the primary. Obama had a total of eighty-seven field offices to Clinton's twenty-seven. Clinton only had field offices in two (Georgia and Tennessee) of the red states voting in the Super Tuesday primaries. In terms of technology, however, the Dean campaign seemed almost prehistoric. At a Center for Politics Post-Election Conference, former Dean campaign strategist Joe Trippi acknowledged that while Bill Clinton's 1992 campaign strategy was based on his adviser James Carville's memorable phrase, 'It's the economy, stupid', the rallying cry for Obama should be 'It's the networks, stupid'. Obama could exploit the advances in the social networking power of the Internet that had occurred in the short space of four years. In Trippi's words, 'Obama just built the biggest network anyone's ever seen. Howard Dean led the Wright Brothers. Barack Obama led Apollo 11.'[117]

Get out the vote

Obama had an additional advantage over the Clinton campaign. Clinton's operatives came largely from her home state of New York and from Washington, DC. Obama hired a number of campaign workers who had worked with congressional campaigns for former House Democratic leader Dick Gephardt of Missouri and former Senate Democratic leader Tom Daschle of South Dakota. They were able to pick up on the Clinton fatigue in the heartland and exploit it to Obama's advantage.

David Plouffe, a former Gephardt operative, was hired as campaign manager. Plouffe orchestrated a long-term strategy that looked beyond the primaries on Super Tuesday, 5 February. The Clinton campaign erroneously thought that she would have clinched the nomination after Super Tuesday. Plouffe's strategy consisted of sending staff to states that the Clinton campaign had largely ignored, particularly the small caucus states. The strategy paid off. Little by little, Obama amassed a delegate lead over Clinton that won him the nomination.[118]

In autumn 2007, Clinton was regarded as the clear front-runner for the nomination. She relished portraying herself as the inevitable candidate with a clear path to the nomination. Obama's surprise win in the first caucus state of Iowa on 3 January 2008 made it clear that the race would likely become protracted and increasingly acrimonious. The Clinton campaign regrouped and managed to win the first primary in New Hampshire on 8 January.

Clinton had, however, based her campaign on wrapping up the nomination by Super Tuesday, 5 February. The Obama campaign had prepared for a longer contest. Towards the end of 2007 it conducted a number of training sessions in all Super Tuesday states. The trainees were then organized into teams divided into congressional districts and were instructed to build effective organizations that would reach individual precincts.[119] Furthermore, Obama managed to recruit staff who, like him, had a background in community organizing. Two of the most important were Marshall Ganz and Temo Figueroa.

Figueroa was hired as the Field Director for the Obama campaign. He was the son of farm worker organizers and had worked as a labour organizer. He was responsible for setting up so-called Camp Obamas in primary states to train volunteers. Figueroa acknowledged the link between Obama's past as a community organizer and the organization he had created to run an effective presidential campaign. As he put it, 'For me, personally as an organizer, coming from labor, it's been an incredible experience to invite mentors of mine – colleagues in labor organizing, community organizing and faith community organizing – to come and be part of truly an inspiring movement . . . And it's a really powerful message to our activists to be trained by some of the same organizations and organizers who trained [Obama].'[120]

Networks

Unlike Figueroa, Ganz held no official position in the Obama campaign. He was, however, something of a legend in community organizing. Ganz, currently a Lecturer in Public Policy at Harvard University's Kennedy School of Government, started his career as a grassroots organizer when Obama was just a child. Like Obama, Ganz was inspired by the work of Saul Alinsky. As an undergraduate student at Harvard in the early 1960s, he had taken leave from his studies to work in Mississippi registering African Americans to vote. In the late 1960s, Ganz was an active supporter of Cesar Chavez's United Farm Workers (UFW). While campaigning in California in 1968, Democratic presidential candidate Robert F. Kennedy came to Delano to show his support for the grape pickers' strike led by Chavez. In turn, Chavez persuaded the UFW to campaign for Kennedy by conducting voter registration and get out the vote campaigns similar to those Obama would later organize in Chicago. Kennedy's commitment to the UFW paid off. According to Chavez, for every Latino who worked for John F. Kennedy in the 1960 campaign, fifty worked for his younger brother in 1968. Kennedy went on to win the California primary. Ganz had arranged for him to speak to a group of farm workers after his victory speech and was at the Ambassador Hotel in Los Angeles in 1968, ready to take him to a rally, when Kennedy was assassinated.[121]

Ganz had been involved in setting up so-called neighbourhood teams for the Sierra Club and brought this experience to the Obama campaign. He conducted training sessions at various Camp Obamas around the country. Central to Ganz's message was the importance for volunteers to convey a sense of moral commitment to a cause instead of merely parroting the candidate's policy positions. Ganz believed that the narrative of the Obama campaign, i.e. the stories it told, were more effective than the endless recitation of the candidate's position on the issues. He urged volunteers to share their life stories with potential voters as a way of creating a bond based on commitment and enthusiasm.[122]

Several groups with no direct affiliation with the Obama campaign became involved in voter registration drives. Perhaps the most prominent was the grassroots organization Association of Community Organizations for Reform Now (ACORN). Formed in 1970, according to its website it 'is the nation's largest grassroots community organization of low- and moderate-income people with over 400,000 member families organized into more than 1,200 neighborhood chapters in 110 cities across the country'.[123] ACORN first garnered national attention for its work in helping to rebuild the devastated 9th Ward in New Orleans in the wake of hurricane Katrina.

In the course of the 2008 campaign, ACORN launched voter registration drives in primarily poor neighbourhoods across the country. The overzealousness of some recruits caused the organization to come under fire from the McCain campaign and conservative talk radio. There had been several instances where enthusiastic volunteers, in their eagerness to submit long lists of voters, had filled out registration cards with names like Mickey Mouse. ACORN regretted these isolated glitches, but pointed out that the names would have been rejected at the polling booth anyway, and there was consequently no justification for John McCain to charge in October 2008 that ACORN was 'is now on the verge of maybe perpetrating one of the greatest frauds in voter history in this country, maybe destroying the fabric of democracy'.[124]

Project Vote, an affiliate of ACORN, had been at the forefront of the registration drives. Since Obama had been head of the local Project Vote office in Chicago in 1992, Republicans sought to link ACORN directly to the Obama campaign. However, Project Vote was an independent grassroots organization during the time Obama worked for it in Chicago. So persistent were the rumours of Obama's affiliation with ACORN that the campaign website set up to respond to false accusations, 'Fight the Smears', posted a page devoted to refuting right-wing claims about ACORN.[125]

The political blogosphere provided another kind of support for Obama, though many progressive sites took him to task for being too eager to compromise in the name of bipartisanship. One of the leading bloggers made no attempt to conceal his political views. The first words that Markos Moulitsas Zuniga wrote when starting his blog *Daily Kos* were: 'I am progressive. I am liberal. I make no apologies.'[126]

The political blogosphere emerged out of the Clinton impeachment and the controversy surrounding the election of 2000, in which George W. Bush lost the popular vote but became president after the Supreme Court, in a 5–4 decision, stopped the recount in Florida. In a sense, it filled the gap left by the decrease of civic and political organizations and benefited from the democraticization of media with the advent of new technologies. However, as *New York Times* journalist Matt Bai discovered, for all its effectiveness in contributing to the ongoing political debate and helping progressive candidates, the netroots culture was stunted by 'a complete disconnect from history'.[127]

Bai is perhaps being too harsh on the bloggers. Zuniga dedicated his book *Taking On the System* to Saul Alinsky and his subtitle, *Rules for Radical Change in a Digital Era*, is clearly meant as a twenty-first-century version of Alinsky's classic *Rules for Radicals*. In any event, the Obama campaign benefited from the support of the political blogosphere – progressive sites like *Daily Kos* and *OpenLeft* endorsed Obama in March 2008 after their preferred candidate, former Senator John Edwards of North Carolina, dropped out of the race. Some tensions, however, emerged during the general election campaign, especially after Obama voted for the Foreign Intelligence Surveillance Act, which mandated retroactive immunity to telecommunications companies, thus making it likely that civil courts would reject lawsuits accusing the Bush administration of civil liberties violations.

Obama's own campaign connected the history and tactics of community organizations with the latest developments in technology. Campaign staff created online networking tools to assist volunteers all over the US in organizing groups in a grassroots get-out-the-vote effort. As one volunteer put it, Obama's web network was 'sort of MeetUp meets Facebook meets MySpace in one area'. The social networking tool my.BarackObama.com, run by Facebook co-founder Chris Hughes, coordinated much of the campaign's grassroots efforts.[128]

Which side are you on?

Obama and the Democratic Party also benefited from the support of labour unions. Organized labour contributed over $100 million to Obama and Democratic congressional candidates. Not surprisingly, organized labour hoped that the Obama administration would deliver on some of their legislative priorities, including universal health care and passage of the Employee Free Choice Act.

During the Harlan County, Kentucky coal miners' strike in 1931, Florence Reece, the wife of a union organizer for the United Mine Workers, penned a song in support of the union cause. 'Which Side Are You On?' with its closing lines, 'Us poor folks haven't got a chance/Unless we organize', became a rallying cry not only for the striking miners in Harlan County, but for the union movement as a whole.

The Democratic Congress chose sides in 1935 by passing the Wagner Act, which President Franklin D. Roosevelt promptly signed, and which guaranteed workers' right to organize unions and bargain collectively. Often called 'labor's Magna Carta', the bill resulted in a surge in union membership. Republicans opposed the bill and, after taking control of Congress in 1946, as part of an attempt to roll back New Deal legislation, passed the Taft–Hartley Act, which sought to reverse the power of unions by making it more difficult to organize.

In spite of Republican efforts, union membership increased from 11.6 per cent of the nonagricultural workforce in 1930 to a high of 34.7 per cent in 1954. In the 1960s, organized labour would play a crucial role in sustaining a liberal economic and political agenda.[129]

Part of the Republican counterrevolution under Ronald Reagan in the 1980s was the blatant attempt to weaken the power of unions. It has often been remarked the beginning of Bill Clinton's presidency was marked by his initiative to permit gays to join the military, which was particularly ill-advised because Clinton had avoided service during the Vietnam War and was therefore perceived by some to lack an understanding of military matters. Ronald Reagan, on the other hand, began his presidency with a forceful show of resolve. In August 1981, the Professional Air Traffic Controllers Organization (PATCO) voted to strike for better wages and benefits. Reagan presented the union members with an ultimatum – either return to work or be fired. When the majority failed to comply, Reagan simply dismissed them and brought in military air personnel to keep planes in the air. Reagan's bold move put organized labour on the defensive and Reagan proceeded to cut programmes dear to unions.

In the 1990s the Clinton administration paid far too little attention to the effects of globalization on the working class. In December 1993 Bill Clinton signed the North American Free Trade Agreement (NAFTA) into law. Its results have largely been detrimental to the interests of American workers. In a 2006 report, the Economic Policy Institute found that the US had lost over a million jobs as a direct result of NAFTA. Furthermore, the report found that NAFTA had 'contributed to the reduction of employment in high-wage, traded-goods industries, the growing inequality in wages, and the steadily declining demand for workers without a college education'.[130]

In the beginning of the 2008 campaign, the three front-runners – Clinton, Edwards and Obama – all supported a renegotiation of the NAFTA. The issue was particularly awkward for Hillary Clinton, who had to distance herself from her husband's enthusiasm for NAFTA while running in part on the memory of his overall record.

Renegotiating NAFTA was widely dismissed as election-year posturing. The Republicans were quick to condemn any talk of renegotiation as appeasement for a protectionist trade policy that would be harmful to US economic interests. The controversy over the future of NAFTA is, however, part of a larger dilemma for the Democratic Party and for the Obama administration – how to avoid protectionist trade policies while maintaining the support of the working class, especially those organized in unions. Obama expressed his belief during the campaign that any trade agreement ought to contain environmental and labour protections. As he put it in a speech at a General Motors plant in Janesville, Wisconsin in February 2008: 'Trade deals like NAFTA and China have been signed with plenty of protections for corporations and their profits, but none for our environment or our workers who've seen factories shut their doors and millions of jobs disappear; workers whose right to organize and unionize has been under assault for the last eight years.'[131]

For, despite the success of Reagan's deunionization campaign, about 25 per cent of the electorate is made up of voters from union households. In certain states, that figure is higher. In Michigan, for example, union households account for 37 per cent of voters.

Obama takes over a US markedly different than that of

the New Deal era. The union movement has changed since its heyday during that era and the nadir of the Reagan years. It has attempted to adapt to the challenges of globalization and the post-industrial economy and to organize more workers in new and growing sectors.

In 2008, the Bureau of Labor Statistics released figures showing that union membership experienced the largest increase since 1979, the year before Reagan was elected.[132] Recent surveys indicate that there remains broad-based support for unions. In a Gallup poll released in December, 2008, 59 per cent of those surveyed said they approved of unions. However, there were stark divisions along party lines. A full 72 per cent of Democrats and a sizeable 63 per cent of independents support labour unions, while only 38 per cent of those identifying themselves as Republicans do so.[133]

On 15 February 2008, shortly after Super Tuesday, the Service Employees International Union (SEIU) endorsed Obama. The SEIU is the fastest-growing union in the US and currently has over 1.9 million members. It is the largest health care and property services union in the country and the second largest public employee union. Obama had a long history with the SEIU. He had close ties with Chicago's SEIU Local 880, working with it both as a community organizer and as an Illinois state senator.

The SEIU announced that it would back up its support for Obama by mobilizing voters using volunteers going door-to-door and working the phones and sending emails, and buying ad time on radio and television.[134] Andy Stern, president of the SEIU, recognized that the union movement cannot simply copy the strategies from a bygone era:

> Of course, we are as far today from the New Deal as the New Deal was from the Civil War. We cannot expect that work will be valued and rewarded in a global economy by reflexively copying strategies from an industrial

economy. Although our values stay the same, our strategies must change.[135]

Stern is a controversial figure. He took SEIU out of the American Federation of Labor and the Congress of Industrial Organizations (AFL-CIO, the largest federation of unions in the US). He believes that, in a globalized economy, labour and business should not continue the adversarial relationship that characterized the 1930s, but should rather work together to solve the economic problems of the twenty-first century. To that end, Stern created Wal-Mart Watch to oversee the nation's largest retailer's treatment of employees. However, Stern has also worked with Wal-Mart founder Sam Walton to end employer-based health care in favour of universal low-cost coverage.

Stern represents a reinvigorated union movement that is pushing hard for universal health care and the implementation of the Employee Free Choice Act (EFCA), which would make it easier for employees to form unions by signing cards authorizing union representation and impose penalties on employers attempting to block such efforts. EFCA has passed in the House of Representatives, but has been stalled in the Senate because of Republican opposition. During the campaign, the SEIU ran an ad featuring Obama expressing his support for the EFCA and saying unequivocally that 'it's time we had a president who honors organized labor, who has walked on picket lines, who doesn't choke on the word union'. He ended by urging voters to 'reclaim the idea that opportunity is open to anyone who is willing to work for it'.[136]

Organized labour contributed $80 million to Obama's campaign because it saw him as a supporter of unions. Some of Obama's early cabinet appointments caused consternation among many on the left. Nominating his main rival for the Democratic nomination, Hillary Clinton, as his Secretary of State, and choosing to retain Robert Gates, a Bush appointee, as Secretary of Defense, were perceived as unnecessary concessions to Clinton supporters within the Democratic Party and a signal that Obama intended to continue the Bush foreign policy of the second term instead of making a clean break with the past.

The fear that Obama was acting too cautiously in choosing his cabinet was somewhat rectified in the eyes of the left with his choice for Secretary of Labor. Hilda Solis was the first Latina to be elected to Congress. She served five terms in the House of Representatives, representing the 32nd congressional district in California that includes East Los Angeles.

Solis's selection was positively received by the union movement for two reasons. She had long been a vocal advocate for EFCA. The EFCA is a top priority for the union movement, which hopes for early passage of the legislation under the new administration. Furthermore, as the daughter of Mexican and Nicaraguan immigrants, Solis also represents one of the fastest growing groups within the labour movement.

Upon first hearing of Obama's choice of Solis, Andy Stern exclaimed, 'It's extraordinary. On every issue that's important to us, she has stood up for an America where everyone's hard work is valued and rewarded.'[137]

Republicans, however, were staunchly opposed to Solis's nomination, primarily because of her support for the EFCA. Senate minority leader Mitch McConnell raised the spectre of Europeanization in connection with a bill he characterized as 'an outrageous proposal. It will fundamentally harm America and Europeanize America and we will have a big political fight over this.'[138] Bernie Marcus, cofounder and former CEO of Home Depot, went one step further and lamented that passage of the Act would be 'the demise of civilization'.[139]

The intention of the bill is the exact opposite of the caricature presented by Republicans and conservative businessmen and pundits. The National Labor Relations Board

(NLRB), an independent federal agency charged with conducting workplace elections for union representation, has been weakened since Roosevelt's day. After workers submit a formal request to organize, the NLRB schedules a secret-ballot vote. In the ensuing month or more, companies are free to hire anti-union consultants and use scare tactics such as spreading rumours that the workplace might close if the union is approved. In such a coercive environment, simply signing cards would facilitate union organization.[140]

The bill passed the House in 2007, but Senate Republicans succeeded in blocking a vote on the bill that year. Solis voted for the bill and Obama expressed his support for it during the campaign. Solis was finally confirmed in February. The Obama administration will likely push to see the EFCA passed in 2009.

The decline of unions after the 1960s cannot be attributed to deindustrialization and the rise of the service economy. Rather, it makes more sense to point to the collusion between antiunionist forces within the Republican Party, starting with the Goldwater insurgency in 1964, and business interests that have worked to suppress labour unions. Just as business and movement conservatism united in the 1980s to mount an offensive against unions, so a president supportive of unions can perhaps help turn the tide of the past decades.

The Europeanization of America or a new New Deal?

Shortly after the Super Tuesday primary elections on 5 February, Republican presidential candidate and former governor of Massachusetts Mitt Romney came to a meeting of the Conservative Political Action Conference (CPAC) in Washington, DC and announced that he was suspending his campaign. In a rambling and at times incoherent speech, he gave his reasons for doing so. Not surprisingly, his poor showing in virtually all the primaries and caucuses in January and February was not among them. He assured his audience that he was stepping aside not because of personal disappointment over the election results, but for the future of the United States.

Romney painted an ominous picture of what lay ahead if the Democrats should win the election in November. He made it clear that if either Hillary Clinton or Barack Obama were to become president, the US would 'surrender to terror'. The choice for Romney was simple: a Republican victory in November would lead to victory in the global war on terror; a Democratic victory would lead to failure and defeat. However, the war on terror was not the only challenge facing the US. Romney spent the bulk of his speech talking about what he saw as the most fundamental challenge – 'the threat to our culture [that] comes from within'. These threats included a culture of poverty brought on by the profligate welfare programmes of the 1960s, the attack on religion – Romney didn't specify who was engaging in these attacks – the rise in sexual promiscuity and the weakening of the institution of marriage by 'unelected judges'.

The erosion of the cultural values that made the US strong and the defeatist attitudes towards the war on terror, both promoted by the insidious forces of the left, portended a grim future for the world's only superpower:

> We face a new generation of challenges, challenges which threaten our prosperity, our security and our future. I am convinced that unless America changes course, we will become the France of the twenty-first century. . .[141]

The prospect of the US degenerating into the pithy status of a European nation was too terrible to contemplate:

> Europe is facing a demographic disaster. That is the inevitable product of weakened faith in the Creator, failed families, disrespect for the sanctity of human life and eroded morality.[142]

Romney's equation of cultural dissolution, demographic suicide and weakened resolve with Europe comported well with conservative anti-European attitudes that have flourished since 9/11. Fear of secularization coupled with imminent Muslim takeover in Europe pervade American conservative discourse in the post-9/11 era.

Much discussion of what to expect from an Obama administration focused on whether he would initiate a new New Deal for the US. Obama himself did nothing to dispel this talk. Indeed, shortly after the election, he gave an interview with *60 Minutes* in which he was asked what he was reading at the moment. Obama replied that he was reading a new book on Franklin D. Roosevelt's 100 days. There was some speculation in the media as to which book he was referring to, given that there were a number of new books on FDR in circulation. It emerged that Obama was in fact reading two FDR books – Jean Edward Smith's recent biography and journalist Jonathan Alter's 2004 *Defining Moment* about the first hundred days of the FDR administration. A cover of *Time* boasted a picture of Obama as FDR, replete with trademark cigarette holder.

Declaring in his inaugural address that 'the nation asks for action and action now', FDR proceeded to deliver just that. In the course of his first three months in office, FDR declared a bank holiday and Congress passed an Emergency Banking Act and the Glass–Steagall Act, which prohibited commercial banks from buying and selling stock. In a desperate effort to provide immediate relief, FDR created jobs to help improve the nation's infrastructure and entered the housing market to protect homeowners from foreclosure. While the first New Deal was primarily devoted to recovery, the second New Deal focused on providing Americans with economic security. FDR established the modern welfare state by creating programmes for unemployment insurance and aid to the poor. The Works Progress Administration continued FDR's policy of infrastructure improvement, hiring millions of Americans to construct buildings, bridges and roads, many of which stand today. The WPA also funded the arts. Woody Guthrie received federal funding to write songs about the construction of the Grand Coulee Dam. Authors were employed to write cultural and travel guides to the forty-eight states.[143]

Unlike FDR, whose New Deal was hastily put together in his first months in office, Obama had the advantage of hindsight. By reading about the New Deal, he could reflect on what worked and what did not. It was clear from the outset that the improvement of the infrastructure would be a major priority for the Obama administration. In 2005, the same year as hurricane Katrina, the American Society of Civil Engineers (ASCE) published a *Report Card for America's Infrastructure*. Four years before Obama took office, the ASCE estimated that it would cost a staggering $1.6 trillion to improve the nation's infrastructure.[144]

The prospect of a new New Deal sparked a lively discussion between conservatives and liberals. Most of the conservative arguments about the failure of the New Deal drew from Amity Shlaes's book *The Forgotten Man*. George Will, conservative columnist for the *Washington Post*, who insisted the New Deal didn't work, quoted Shlaes approvingly in his column. Liberals, on the other hand, were quick to point out that the New Deal was in fact successful during its first years. An exchange between Will and liberal columnist and economist Paul Krugman, on the Sunday morning programme *ABC This Week* in late November 2008, encapsulated the two viewpoints. Will repeated the conservative line that FDR turned the depression into a Great Depression. Krugman countered that the economy improved between 1933 and 1937 and it was only when FDR decided to cut spending in 1937 that the economy took a downturn.[145]

In *The Age of Reform*, Richard Hofstadter observed that the New Deal had given 'a social democratic tinge' to the

US.[146] As Romney warned, European-style collectivism has made a comeback. Bush was roundly criticized for his slow reaction to the aftermath of hurricane Katrina in 2005. Leading figures in the Democratic Party, including Senator Edward Kennedy and former Senator John Edwards, called for the establishment of New Deal-like initiatives such as jobs programmes and a Gulf Coast Regional Development Authority to help in the reconstruction of the devastated areas along the Gulf Coast.[147] The failure of the Coolidge administration to react swiftly and effectively after the Louisiana flood of 1927 changed the way Americans regarded the role of the federal government. In the wake of the flood, many Americans felt that the federal government had a responsibility to help individual citizens. This shift in attitude helped pave the way for the New Deal.[148] The devastation of Katrina and the Bush administration's slow and woefully inadequate response may well have had a similar effect eighty years later.

Just how out of touch the Republican right wing was with shifts in public opinion towards the role of government was abundantly evident in the response that Louisiana's Governor Bobby Jindal, widely regarded as a possible GOP candidate in 2012, gave to Obama's first address to Congress in February 2009. Jindal had turned down $100 million in federal funding to his state – which ranks fourth in children living below the poverty line and forty-sixth in high school graduation rates – as part of the stimulus package. He cited hurricane Katrina not as an example of the dangers of too little government, but too much. According to Jindal, it was government bureaucracy that prevented aid in reaching New Orleans in time, not government incompetence.[149]

Democrats as well as Republicans see health care reform as a wedge issue that has profound implications for the future of the US. At the beginning of 1994, William Kristol wrote an op-ed in the *Wall Street Journal*, in which he urged Republican senators and congressmen to mount a

spirited offensive against the health care reform proposals put forward by the Clinton administration. As Kristol
argued, 'Passage of the Clinton health care plan *in any
form* would be disastrous. It would guarantee an unprecedented federal intrusion into the American economy. Its
success would signal the rebirth of centralized welfare-state
policy.'[150] Bush would seem to agree with this assessment.
In vetoing the SCHIP bill (State Children's Health Insurance
Program) which would have expanded health care services
to children, Bush insisted that

> What you're seeing when you expand eligibility for
> federal programs is the desire by some in Washington,
> DC to federalize health care. I don't think that's good for
> the country.[151]

Other leading conservatives expressed their concern about
the decline of conservatism in terms similar to Romney's.
A cover story in *The National Review* carried the ominous
headline, 'The Coming Cataclysm'. In the accompanying
article, entitled appropriately 'The Grim Truth', Ramesh
Ponnuru and Richard Lowry argued that a Democratic
victory in November

> would probably also mean a national health-insurance
> program that would irrevocably expand government
> involvement in the economy and American life, and itself
> make voters less likely to turn toward conservatism in the
> future.[152]

In a comment on this doomsday scenario, *New York Times*
columnist Paul Krugman cheerily suggested that 'the implications of universal coverage would extend far beyond
health care, that it would revitalize the New Deal idea.'[153]

On 4 February 2009, Obama signed into law the so-called
SCHIP bill that extended health insurance to low-income

children. The original SCHIP programme dates back to 1997 and was aimed at providing health insurance to children from families who earned too much to qualify for Medicaid, but did not earn enough to afford adequate health insurance.

After the 2006 mid-term elections the Democrats, emboldened by their sizeable majority in both houses of Congress, decided to push for an expansion of the original SCHIP programme. The legislation encountered staunch opposition by Republicans in Congress and in the White House. In 2007 Bush vetoed legislation that would have increased the number of children covered by SCHIP from 6.6 million to 10 million. At a news conference before vetoing the bill, Bush expressed concern that the proposed legislation would be a step towards 'government-run health care for every American'.[154]

Even though several Republican lawmakers ended up voting for the bill in 2009, Republicans opposed to the bill voiced concerns similar to those of Bush. Representative Steve King, Republican of Iowa, regarded the bill as nothing less than 'a foundation stone for socialized medicine'.[155]

Obama took an entirely different view of the bill. At the signing ceremony he said:

> We're not a nation that leaves struggling families to fend for themselves, especially when they've done everything right. No child in America should be receiving his or her primary care in the emergency room in the middle of the night. No child should be falling behind at school because he can't hear the teacher or see the blackboard.
>
> I refuse to accept that millions of our children fail to reach their full potential because we fail to meet their basic needs. In a decent society, there are certain obligations that are not subject to tradeoffs or negotiations, and health care for our children is one of those obligations.[156]

Some Republicans did vote for the bill. Most, however, saw it as a slippery slope towards what they called 'the government-run-health-care agenda'. Their fears that the SCHIP bill might be the first step towards national health insurance were warranted. In the federal budget which the Obama administration released a little over a month after he took office, $634 billion was set aside for comprehensive health care reform. The money would be raised by abolishing deductions for families making more than $250,000 a year and cutting federal subsidies for insurance companies that administer Medicare programmes.

In his weekly radio address on 28 February 2009, Obama was emphatic in underscoring his willingness to take up the fight against those who would oppose his budget proposals, including health care reform. As he put it, 'I know they're gearing up for a fight as we speak. My message to them is this: So am I.'[157]

Liberal groups and unions, working together with businesses, were also gearing up for the fight. The Center for American Progress, a group formed by former Clinton chief-of-staff and the director of Obama's transition team John Podesta, founded Better Health Care Together with SEIU president Andy Stern. Leading businesses like Wal-Mart and AT&T are also members of Better Health Care Together.[158] This close cooperation between business, liberal organizations and labour will likely increase Obama's chances for passing comprehensive health care reform.

If the Bush administration could be characterized as the apogee of the Southernization of American politics, the proposals for health care reform and a multilateral foreign policy relying on diplomatic rather than military solutions to international crises would seem to augur the return to the Europeanization of American politics of the Roosevelt era of activist government and liberal internationalism.

In this sense, Mitt Romney was right. A Democratic victory and the impending demise of the conservative movement may well lead to the US becoming more like Europe. That being said, there is no reason to assume that the transatlantic discord that characterized the relations between the US and a number of EU nations during Bush's tenure will be resolved overnight. Hillary Clinton and Barack Obama's health care proposals maintain a reliance on insurance companies that would be anathema in many European nations. Their essays in *Foreign Affairs* leave no doubt that the US should be the leader in world affairs and tend towards narratives of national greatness not totally devoid of hubris – even though there are clear gestures towards liberal internationalism.

But for conservatives, the narrowing Atlantic gap is cause for concern, if not outright hysteria. As Jonah Goldberg put it in *The National Review* in 2005, 'if you're worried about the Europeanization of America, let me quote from the original *Body Snatchers*: "They're here already! You're next! You're next! You're next . . ."'[159]

The Obama administration's economic stimulus plan convinced many conservatives that the US was indeed next in line for Europeanization. In urging House Republican Mike Pence of Indiana to do everything in his power to prevent Obama's bill from being passed, conservative *Fox News* commentator Sean Hannity called the legislation 'the European Socialist Act of 2009'.[160] Republican Senate minority leader Mitch McConnell of Kentucky echoed Hannity's fears. Passing the stimulus bill, McConnell warned, would constitute 'a dramatic move in the direction of indeed turning America into Western Europe.'[161]

Not all Republicans were apprehensive about the possible Europeanization of America, at least not in some areas. The prospect of the nationalization of banks as part of Secretary of the Treasury Tim Geithner's plan to rescue the US financial system became very real in the first months of 2009. In several interviews, Obama would not rule out following the Swedish model of nationalizing the banks from the 1990s, but he hedged a bit, saying that the solution was more viable in a small country like Sweden with fewer banks than in the US, which has thousands of financial institutions. He received support for this view from an unexpected quarter. Senator Lindsey Graham (R-SC) let it be known that he, too, was not averse from adopting a financial rescue plan that proved successful in a social democratic society like Sweden.[162]

Organizing for America

On Saturday, 17 January 2009, just before he embarked on a train trip from Philadelphia to Washington, DC, Obama announced that his campaign, Obama for America, would be transformed into Organizing for America and would build on 'the largest grass roots movement in history'. The organization would be comprised of '[v]olunteers, grass roots leaders and ordinary citizens' and would serve to mobilize public support for his policies.[163]

The first test of Organizing for America was not long in coming. A top priority for the incoming Obama administration was to pass an economic stimulus package. An early version of the bill passed the House, but did not receive any Republican votes. The strict party vote flew in the face of the post-partisan rhetoric that Obama had voiced to much acclaim in his 2004 Democratic Convention speech (which had motivated his candidacy). Immediately after the vote, the media was full of debate about the viability of Obama's vision of One America. When pressed, however, Obama himself was not above playing the partisan card. Just days after he took office, he met with congressional leaders in an effort to garner bipartisan support for his stimulus bill. When Republicans started to complain about what they believed was unnecessary spending in the bill, Obama was quick to remind them that, as he put it, 'I won.'

House Republicans had two reasons for opposing the

bill – tactical and ideological. They seemed to be following the lead of an influential outsider, the radio talk show host Rush Limbaugh, who in a broadcast made no secret of his contempt for Obama and his stimulus bill. 'I hope he fails,' railed Limbaugh, who was portrayed in the press as the de facto Republican leader. House Republicans reasoned that if Obama did fail, they would come out ahead in the mid-term elections in 2010, not having in any way been responsible if the economy did not respond to the stimulus.

However, the anti-New Deal ideology that had been a mainstay of the Grand Old Party for so long was also a motivating factor for Republican opposition. As Paul Krugman put it succinctly in a column, 'Conservatives really, really don't want to see a second New Deal, and they certainly don't want to see government activism vindicated.'[164] All the wrangling about the size of the stimulus package and the extent to which Obama should reach out to Republicans revolved around this salient fact.

In any event, the director of Organizing for America, Mitch Stewart, sent out an email asking those who held house meetings to host Economic Recovery House Meetings on the weekend of 6 February 2009. Organizing for America made online stimulus house party kits, with talking points and a video, available to prospective hosts.[165]

Obama himself seemed to vacillate between being overly conciliatory towards the Republicans and standing his ground against them, accusing them in effect of clinging to shopworn rhetoric and failed economic policies. At a House Democratic Caucus Issues Conference in Williamsburg, Virginia on 5 February 2009, he excoriated Republicans for embracing 'the losing formula that says only tax cuts will work for every problem we face.' To hearty laughter from the audience, he mocked the GOP members of Congress for complaining that 'this is not a stimulus bill, this is a spending bill. What do you think a stimulus is? That's the whole point.'[166] On Friday, 13 February 2009, the largest stimulus bill in American history passed both houses of Congress and was ready for the president's signature. The bill had been pared down to $787 billion from earlier versions of over $800 billion and was a mix of tax cuts and government spending. Thirteen years after a Democratic president, Bill Clinton, had announced that 'the era of big government is over', the stimulus bill signalled a return of big government programmes in energy, education, health care and aid to the unemployed and poor.

Energy efficiency and renewable energy ideas, including weatherizing houses, modernization of the electric grid, and tax incentives for renewable energy such as solar and wind, received $45 billion. The bill included $20 billion for food stamps, a Great Society initiative, as well as an extra $25 a week for those receiving unemployment benefits, and one-time payments of $250 for recipients of Social Security and veterans' benefits. The Great Society programme Head Start, set up as part of President Lyndon B. Johnson's war on poverty, providing education and nutrition services to low-income children, received $2.1 billion. Public schools, universities and day-care centres received $100 billion over two years. Another Great Society programme, Medicaid, providing health care services to the poor, was given $87 billion in federal funds to the states. The bill mandated $120 billion in public works projects to improve the American infrastructure, twice the amount that Obama had campaigned for. Tax cuts to individuals and businesses made up 35 per cent of the bill, or about $282 billion.

In less than a month after taking office, Obama had pushed through a federally funded stimulus plan that could be characterized as the coming of the new New Deal. It also contained provisions for increasing funding for programmes set up during LBJ's Great Society. Curiously, the debate about the role of the federal government between conservatives and liberals had revolved around the efficacy of the New Deal. The Great Society had received barely a mention. Obama had little desire to remind Americans of the Johnson years, presumably because LBJ was associated with liberal overreach and the debacle of the Vietnam War. Nevertheless, hidden deep within the 1,000+ pages of the stimulus bill were the Great Society programmes listed above that were the beneficiaries of government largesse.

For all his efforts at outreach, Obama could not bridge the partisan divide. No House Republicans voted for the bill, and only three moderate Republicans in the Senate did so.[167]

Despite the conspicuous lack of bipartisan support, Obama did not veer from his course. The week after he signed the stimulus bill into law, Obama addressed both houses of Congress in a nationally televised speech. The speech was an ill-concealed critique of the policies of the previous administration and the ideology that drove it. Even though he assured Americans that he did not believe in big government, his address focused on public investment in health care, renewable energy and education.

Obama repeated his pledge to make sure that every American had affordable health care. He urged Congress to pass legislation setting caps on carbon pollution and promoting alternative forms of energy. He suggested that more regulation was necessary to prevent car manufacturers from becoming victims of their own bad practices and envisioned 'a re-tooled, re-imagined auto industry'. In keeping with his long-standing support for public service, Obama proposed that the government would reward those who performed some kind of community service with the promise of a higher education.[168]

Obama emphasized that the US stood now at the crossroads of history. His vision for the future nevertheless recalled a bygone past. He was in effect proposing a continuation of the government activism that had characterized the New Deal and the Great Society. Unlike the

Republican counterrevolution of the past three decades, which had attempted to dismantle the achievements of the New Deal era, the new Obama administration seemed intent on renewing the pact between the American people and their government and building on the work of FDR and LBJ.

Two days after his speech, Obama presented the federal budget, which contained sweeping proposals designed to reverse the marked increase in inequality in the US over the past thirty years. During the New Deal era from the 1930s to the 1960s, inequality decreased and the middle class grew. Not everyone benefited from this growth, however. LBJ's Great Society programmes were implemented in an effort to reach what Michael Harrington in 1962 had called 'the other America' in his book of the same name. The Reagan counterrevolution and the rise of trickle-down economics had reversed this course. With the middle class as well as the poor threatened by the economic crisis, Obama's budget was a conscious effort – in his speech he called it not only a blueprint, but a vision for the future of America – to shape a future society based on economic growth, equal opportunity and greater social and economic equality.

As Obama outlined in his speech, the budget focused on health care reform, education reform and energy. To help pay for the massive government outlays necessary for reform, the budget contained concrete proposals for a rewriting of the tax code that would drastically reduce income inequality.

Income inequality plummeted from the late 1930s to the late 1970s. In the 1970s, the top 1 per cent of Americans took home 8 per cent of total income. When Ronald Reagan was elected in 1980, the figure had only increased by 1 per cent. By 2007, however, the top 1 per cent took home over 22 per cent.[169]

Obama's budget put forward a progressive tax that would raise taxes on those making more than $250,000 a year and lower taxes for the rest of Americans. This budget proposal displayed a remarkable continuity with what Obama said on the campaign trail. His exchange with Joe the Plumber was a simplified version of what became part of the budget.

At time of writing, it is of course premature to assess exactly how Obama will govern. However, early indications are that he will pursue his agenda aggressively, while continuing to urge a spirit of volunteerism that he himself learned and benefited from as a community organizer in Chicago.

A change election?

Obama won a substantial electoral victory in November 2008. He was the first Democratic presidential candidate since Jimmy Carter in 1976 to receive over 50 per cent of votes cast. Although he came nowhere near Johnson's landslide in 1964, he did manage to win more than twice as many electoral votes as his opponent, John McCain. Obama won 53 per cent (365 electoral votes) to McCain's 46 per cent (173 electoral votes). He made inroads in the Republican South, winning Florida, North Carolina and Virginia. Virginia had not voted Democrat since 1964. In the West, he added Nevada, Colorado and New Mexico to the solid Democratic coastal states.

In 1968, a young Republican strategist circulated a memo that came to be used as a blueprint for the Republican presidential campaign of Richard Nixon. In 'Middle America and the Emerging Republican Majority', Kevin Phillips argued that with the right political strategy, Republicans could dominate American politics for generations to come. Central to Phillips's strategy proposals was an emphasis on the politics of resentment. He pointed out that the Democrats had effectively used the resentment of economic elites during the Great Depression to forge a lasting coalition.[170]

Phillips expanded his memo into a book the year after the election. Phillips saw the election of 1968 as a reversal and repudiation of the Democratic landslide accorded Lyndon B. Johnson just four years previously. Johnson's overwhelming victory of 61.1 per cent was matched by what Phillips saw as the 'anti-Democratic' vote received by Nixon and third party candidate George Wallace. Together, they garnered 57 per cent of the vote, a sizeable majority. The reorientation of the Republican Party had a regional dimension away from the Northeast and towards the South and West. Phillips traced this trend back to 1948, when the breakaway Dixiecrat party led by Strom Thurmond left the Democratic Convention, incensed by Minneapolis Mayor Hubert Humphrey's speech asking the delegates to support President Harry S Truman in his fight for Civil Rights. As Humphrey put it,

> to those who say that we are rushing this issue of civil rights, I say to them we are 172 years late. To those who say that this civil-rights program is an infringement on states' rights, I say this: The time has arrived in America for the Democratic Party to get out of the shadow of states' rights and to walk forthrightly into the bright sunshine of human rights.[171]

Race was then at the heart of this development. As Phillips put it, 'Now that the *national* Democratic Party is becoming the Negro party throughout most of the South, the alienation of white Wallace voters is likely to persist.'[172] For Phillips, 1968 was the beginning of a new era in American politics. The task for the Republican Party, in his view, was to fashion a long-term majority out of the 57 per cent who voted for Nixon and Wallace in 1968.[173] In one the many maps that dot the text, Phillips sketched the emerging Republican majority.[174] The Plains and Mountain states, the outer South and Texas formed the bastions of Republican strength, with the Deep South a potential Republican region barring the resilience of any third-party movements. Battleground areas consisted of the Pacific, the Ohio–Mississippi Valley and the non-Yankee Northeast. The Democrats were left with Michigan, New York and New England. The map was remarkably prescient. Phillips could hardly have predicted the aftereffect of the Watergate scandal that in effect created Jimmy Carter. The landslide victories of Nixon in 1972 and Reagan in 1984 did not only put Phillips's bastions, the Deep South and most of the battleground states, into the Republican column. Massachusetts was the lone New England state that went to George McGovern in 1972. And in 1984, Walter Mondale managed only to win his home state Minnesota which Phillips had described, along with Iowa and Wisconsin, as a state where 'the GOP is not on the upswing'.[175]

However, over thirty years after Phillips, two political scientists were claiming that developments in the new century were reversing Phillips's old Republican majority. John Judis and Ruy Texeira acknowledged that Phillips had correctly predicted the swing towards the Republican Party after 1968. They contended that the era of the Republican majority was over and that the Democratic Party would become the dominant party in the future. They based their analysis on demographic, economic, geographic and political data. In *The Emerging Democratic Majority*, they predicted that a coalition of women, professionals and minorities living for the most part in what Judis and Texeira called 'ideopolises' (defined as large post-industrial metropolitan areas that merge city and suburb) would form a viable Democratic majority.[176]

In assessing Obama's victory the day after the election, Judis revised the original blueprint for the emerging Democratic majority. '[Obama's] election is the culmination of a Democratic realignment that began in the 1990s, was delayed by September 11, and resumed with the 2006 election.'[177] After the 2006 mid-term election, Judis and Texeira added two new groups to their equation – younger voters and independents.[178]

Obama had a thirteen-point edge over McCain among women, and among people with advanced degrees he won by 58 per cent to 40 per cent. His showing among minorities was impressive by any measure. Not surprisingly, Obama won 96 per cent of the African American vote. He did very well among other minorities, winning 66 per cent of the Latino vote to McCain's 31 per cent and 64 per cent of the Asian vote to McCain's 35 per cent. In 1972, minorities made up only 10 per cent of the electorate. In 2008, they made up 26 per cent.

Turnout among young voters was widely expected to rise in 2008, but the increase from 2004 was negligible. However, voters from 18 to 29 voted overwhelmingly for Obama (66 per cent to McCain's 31 per cent). Younger voters are more supportive of activist government and oppose the war in Iraq. A third of this age group call themselves liberals.[179]

These voting groups form the basis for a progressive Democratic majority. A poll conducted by the Campaign for America's Future and Democracy Corps on the eve of the election found that moderates joined with liberals to form a majority that marginalized conservatives. By substantial margins, both liberals and moderates support government regulation, public investment and alliances with other nations instead of military solutions to national security issues.[180]

Even conservatives agree with this analysis. Mitch McConnell, Republican from Kentucky and Senate minority leader, lamented to the Republican National Committee shortly after Obama's inauguration, 'The Republican Party seems to be slipping into a position of being more of a regional party than a national one.' He put the party's minority status in stark terms. 'You can walk from Canada to Mexico and from Maine to Arizona without ever leaving a state with a Democratic governor. Not a single Republican senator represents the tens of millions of Americans on the West Coast. And on the East Coast, you can drive from North Carolina to New Hampshire without touching a single state in between that has a Republican in the U.S. Senate.' Many moderate Republicans had lost their seats in Congress in the 2008 election, so McConnell's solution to the Republican dilemma was not surprising. He called on his fellow party members to make a better effort at communicating Republican principles instead of changing them, as some Republicans have advocated.[181]

In their study of progressive change in the 1960s, G. Calvin Mackenzie and Robert Weisbrot go against conventional wisdom, which tends to attribute change in that tumultuous decade to protest movements and the counterculture. They mount an argument that 'the dissidents and politicians were in this together' and that 'it was often the very targets of [the protesters'] wrath – the institutions of national politics and the politicians and bureaucrats who inhabited them – that produced the social and economic changes that have become the deep and enduring legacy of the 1960s.'[182]

Politics in the 1960s was, in their view, not simply a bottom–up or for that matter a top–down enterprise, but rather the product of a symbiotic relationship between grassroots movements and those in government. Together they produced a 'liberal hour' that, however short-lived, transformed American society.

Obama came out of a grassroots movement to become the first African American president of the US. He has attempted to bring the tactics he learned as a community organizer in Chicago to the task of organizing America for substantive change.

The question is whether President Barack Obama will be able to sustain the symbiotic relationship he has attempted to forge between the grassroots who helped elect him and the government he is now in charge of. The election of 2008 was both a repudiation of the Bush administration as well as a longing for change. It does not in and of itself constitute a realignment of the American political landscape, even though there is evidence that the nation is trending leftward. However, if Obama succeeds in implementing his own version of the New Deal with the support and, over time, the expansion of the emerging Democratic majority, he may well go down in history as a transformative president.

Part Two
Obama's World

4
At Home in the World

The US from the outside

Even at this early stage of Obama's presidency, the bare outline of an Obama Doctrine, defined as a coherent worldview informing the formulation of a twenty-first-century foreign policy, is discernible. It can be traced back to Obama's formative years and is linked with the development of his identity.

Obama himself has often made the connection between his life story and his foreign policy views. In an interview with James Traub published one year to the day before the election of 2008, Obama made a point of explaining how his biography could make a difference in the way the US was perceived around the globe.

> I think that if you can tell people, 'We have a president in the White House who still has a grandmother living in a hut on the shores of Lake Victoria and has a sister who's half-Indonesian, married to a Chinese-Canadian,' then they're going to think that he may have a better sense of what's going on in our lives and in our country. And they'd be right.[1]

Obama gave his first interview as president to the Arabic television news channel network Al-Arabiya. He was the first president to mention Muslims in his inaugural address, and in the interview he reiterated his desire for outreach to the Muslim world. Emphasizing that 'the language we use has to be a language of respect,' he added, as if to underscore the notion that personal experience matters in foreign policy, that 'I have Muslim members of my family. I have lived in Muslim countries.'[2] During the campaign, Obama's attempt to make the case that his life story provided him with greater insight into foreign affairs than his main rival for the Democratic nomination became the object of some contention.

In March 2008, the Clinton campaign had mounted a relentless offensive against Obama for his lack of foreign policy experience. As the former First Lady, Hillary Clinton reminded voters of the many trips she had taken abroad where she had met with many world leaders. She erroneously hinted that she had had a hand in the peace process in Northern Ireland and, in one embarrassing gaffe, claimed to recall that she had landed in Bosnia in 1996 while under fire from snipers. Clinton released an advert intended to instil confidence in her leadership skills and at the same time sow doubt about her opponent's readiness to undertake the foreign policy challenges that lay ahead.

In the ad, sleeping children and the sound of a phone ringing is accompanied by a sombre voiceover setting the scene. It's 3 a.m., there's a crisis in the world and the question is who would you like answering the phone in this time of need – someone already familiar with foreign leaders or someone new on the world stage? An image of Hillary Clinton with glasses and phone to her ear, alert and clearly vigilant, ends the spot. The message is clear. She has the experience necessary to deal with foreign crises any time of the day.

Although hardly as hard-hitting as LBJs infamous 'Daisy'

ad from 1964, showing a young girl plucking petals from a daisy while counting, interrupted by a grim voice calling out a countdown, followed by an atomic bomb explosion, the Clinton ad had the intended effect of calling Obama's qualifications to be Commander-in-Chief into question.

In order to undercut the argument that he was singularly unprepared to take office as president given his dearth of foreign policy experience, Obama countered by questioning the value of official junkets to foreign countries. He hinted that such trips, the itinerary of which was often controlled by the hosts, gave only superficial insight into foreign cultures. Obama claimed that he had another kind of experience, ultimately more valuable than that gained from official visits. Having lived and travelled in Asia and in Africa, he had the kind of deep knowledge about foreign cultures that was essential for making sound judgements on foreign policy.

> If you don't understand these cultures then it's very hard for you to make good foreign policy decisions. Foreign policy is all about judgment.

Clinton pounced on these remarks:

> Voters will have to judge if living in a foreign country at the age of ten prepares one to face the big, complex international challenges the next president will face. I think we need a president with more experience than that, someone the rest of the world knows, looks up to and has confidence in.[3]

A respected foreign policy analyst came to Obama's defence. Fareed Zakaria, the international editor of *Newsweek* and an immigrant from India, offered his own background as a reason why identity can trump experience and expertise. As Zakaria pointed out, when I think about what is truly distinctive about the way I look at the world, about the advantage that I may have over others in understanding foreign affairs, it is that *I know what it means not to be an American*. I know intimately the attraction, the repulsion, the hopes, the disappointments that the other 95 percent of humanity feels when thinking about this country. I know it because for a good part of my life, I wasn't an American. I was the outsider, growing up 8,000 miles away from the centers of power, being shaped by forces over which my country had no control.[4]

Obama may not have the depth of Zakaria's experience of living in another country for a considerable length of time and coming to the US as an immigrant. However, it is worth remembering that his father had only been in the US for two years when Obama was born. Furthermore, Obama grew up on two Pacific archipelagos – one, Hawaii, which was subject to the first overthrow or regime change by the US in 1893, the other, Indonesia, which hosted the non-aligned movement in 1955, just a little over a decade before Obama came to live there. In his autobiography, Obama mentions that while studying at Occidental College, he gravitated towards politically active black students, Chicano students, and foreign students. He recounts how he and his friends talked late into the night about 'neocolonialism, Franz Fanon, Eurocentrism, and patriarchy'.[5] His first foray into politics was the anti-apartheid movement at Occidental. As an article in *Newsweek* contrasting the worldviews of McCain and Obama put it: 'The success of the antiapartheid movement shaped Obama's views on how to tackle problems that don't lend themselves to military solutions.'[6] To that end, candidate Obama stressed the concept of 'dignity promotion' in foreign policy, which seeks to improve social and economic conditions instead of focusing on holding elections.

Obama's life experiences differ markedly from those of his predecessors. In his inaugural address, John F. Kennedy, born in 1917, a month after the US entered World War I, proclaimed that 'the torch has been passed to a new generation of Americans – born in this century, tempered by war, disciplined by a hard and bitter peace, proud of our ancient heritage'. In the summer of 1937, twenty-year-old John F. Kennedy went on an extended tour of Europe. His travels were part of a well-rounded education for a young man educated at the best schools in the Northeast. Kennedy would travel to Europe several times during the next few years and would write his senior thesis on the origins of British appeasement policy towards Germany in the 1930s, which was later published as *Why England Slept*.[7] Kennedy's focus on Europe resembled that of much of the Establishment that exerted a profound influence on the formulation of American foreign policy from the Spanish–American War to the Vietnam War. The worldview of the Establishment emanated from the East coast and was primarily oriented towards Europe.[8]

The origins of Ronald Reagan's worldview lay elsewhere, however. He was heavily influenced by the right-wing Republicanism of the Midwestern heartland in the 1950s. Midwestern Republicans regarded Europe as corrupt and decadent and believed that close transatlantic ties benefited the Anglophile elite of the East coast. They looked towards the inferior Caribbean and the Pacific as proving grounds for an American civilizing mission. Their worldview had implications for military policy as well. While the Democrats, the party of European immigrants, preferred land wars and were open to compromise and negotiation, the Midwestern Republicans were enamoured of sea and air power. The projection of military power from a distance was arguably the reason why Reagan became fascinated with the so-called Star Wars project in the 1980s.[9]

Obama's immediate predecessor, George W. Bush,

displayed little interest in foreign policy before he became president. Unlike his father, whose foreign policy in some respects harked back to the more traditional internationalism of the pre-Reagan era, George W. Bush was steeped in a tradition of Southern militarism that was aggressive and unilateralist and comported well with the neoconservative ideology of some of his closest advisers.[10]

A son of Africa in the Pacific world

Obama's background and intellectual development attest to an experience with foreign cultures and a keen interest in foreign policy issues. He represents a break both with the transatlantic focus of the Eastern Establishment and the unilateralism and Pacific and Caribbean imperialist orientation of Southern and Western conservatism. Obama spent the first eighteen years of his life on archipelagos in the Pacific, thousands of miles away from the US mainland. He was born in Hawaii in 1961; his mother, Stanley Ann Dunham, had moved there in 1960 with her parents. They had lived in Kansas but had travelled to Texas and Washington state to find work before settling in Hawaii. Obama lived in Indonesia from 1967 to 1971 before returning to Hawaii where he remained until 1979 when he left Hawaii to attend college in California.

Hawaii had gained statehood as the last state in the US the year before the Dunham family arrived. For the Dunhams, who had travelled ever westward, resettling in the new state had an aura of the frontier about it. Hawaii was new in another respect as well. It is the only state in the US to have had a majority–minority population since gaining statehood. According to US Census Bureau data from 1960, the year the Dunhams arrived, the population of Hawaii was 642,000. Whites were less than one third of the population; Asians and Pacific Islanders comprised over two thirds.[11]

Obama's father left when he was only two years old. His

mother subsequently married an Indonesian, Lolo Soetero, in 1967. That same year she accompanied him to Indonesia with her young son. Like Obama's father, Soetero had also been sponsored by his government to study abroad. Indonesia had declared independence from the Netherlands in 1945. Civil violence against the radical government of Sukarno, who had developed close ties with the Soviet Union and the People's Republic of China, was rampant in the years immediately preceding Obama's arrival. The military, led by Major General Suharto, deposed Sukarno in 1967, the year Obama arrived.

Another African American had come to the Asian archipelago in 1955 to attend the first meeting of what became the non-aligned movement. Twenty-nine mostly newly independent countries from Asian and Africa were represented at Bandung, Indonesia. Obama expressed his admiration for the work of his fellow Chicagoan Richard Wright in *Dreams from My Father*. Wright read of the impending meeting in Bandung and could hardly contain his excitement:

The despised, the insulted, the hurt, the dispossessed – in short, the underdogs of the human race were meeting. Here were class and racial and religious consciousness on a global scale . . . And what had these nations in common? Nothing, it seemed to me, but what their past relationship to the Western world had made them feel. This meeting of the rejected was in itself a kind of judgment upon that Western world![12]

Wright was no less enthusiastic upon leaving Bandung, expressing his hope that the unity of purpose he saw there would engender the 'shaking loose of the Asian-African masses from a static past'.

The Bandung Conference was notable because it sought to go beyond the Manichean division of the world between East and West during the Cold War and develop what came to be called a Third World perspective on geopolitical events. Even though Obama has never mentioned reading this particular work of Wright, it is probable that he at least was aware of it, given his experience in Indonesia and his later interest in questions of decolonization and national liberation.

Soetero worked for an American oil company in Indonesia while Obama's mother pursued a degree in anthropology. Her doctoral dissertation from 1992, 'Peasant blacksmithing in Indonesia: surviving against all odds', was a study of the resilience of village industries in the face of encroaching urbanization. While working on her dissertation, she landed a job as a consultant for the United States Agency for International Development (USAID), working on setting up a village credit programme. She then worked as a Ford Foundation programme officer specializing in women's work in the capital, Jakarta. In the 1980s she helped build microfinance programmes in Indonesia, which is now number one in terms of savers. For a brief time she was a microfinance consultant in Pakistan, then returned to Indonesia to work in the country's oldest bank on its microfinance programme. Her work brought her back to the American mainland. In the 1990s she worked at Women's World Banking, an international network of microfinance providers.[13]

Microfinance has in recent years received a great deal of publicity, not least through the work of Muhammad Yunus, the creator of Grameen Bank. Yunus won the Nobel Peace Prize in 2006. His mother's work in microfinance clearly made a lasting impression on Obama. In her opening statement at the Senate hearings on her nomination as Secretary of State, Hillary Clinton spoke of her own work in microfinance and paid tribute to Obama's mother.

I want to mention that President-elect Obama's mother, Ann Dunham, was a pioneer in microfinance in Indonesia

... [H]er work in international development, the care and concern she showed for women and for poor people around the world, mattered greatly to her son, and certainly has informed his views and his vision. We will be honored to carry on Ann Dunham's work in the months and years ahead.[14]

Shortly after her confirmation, the new Secretary of State met with employees of USAID, the agency that Ann Dunham had worked for in Indonesia. Clinton mentioned her talks with Yunus and once again praised Dunham's work in microfinance and how it had deepened Obama's 'understanding and commitment to these important human issues'.[15]

Obama recorded his first impressions of Indonesia in his autobiography. By his own account, he learned its language and traditions quickly. His mother learned of the circumstances surrounding the military coup in Indonesia from teaching English to Indonesian businessmen at the US Embassy. Obama recalls how his mother had been frightened to discover how 'history could be swallowed up so completely . . . as if nothing had happened'. Living in a poor, underdeveloped country, Obama learned from his mother to 'disdain the blend of ignorance and arrogance that too often characterized Americans abroad'. She was nevertheless determined that her son be an American. Her Americanism was of a particular sort, however. According to Obama, she was a 'lonely witness for secular humanism, a soldier for New Deal, Peace Corps, position-paper liberalism'. Part of his Americanism, she decided, would be as an African American. To that end, she provided him with a steady diet of the history of the Civil Rights movement, African American music and literature.[16]

His experience in Indonesia stayed with him. In a revealing passage in *Dreams from My Father*, he compares the economically depressed areas of Chicago with the slums of

Jakarta. A glimpse of a Korean woman sewing by hand with a sleeping child beside her in a clothing store near Altgeld Gardens in Chicago transports Obama back to the markets in Jakarta. He muses that, despite the rampant poverty in Indonesia, the lives of the venders in Jakarta had at least some semblance of coherence and order that was sorely lacking in the Chicago ghetto.[17]

In his autobiography, he recounts his childhood in Hawaii in terms of his search for identity. Even though interracial marriage was fairly common on the islands, it occurred primarily between Asians and European Americans. His Kansan mother's union with a Kenyan man was highly unusual. The African American population of Hawaii was negligible at the time and is only 2.5 per cent today.

Upon returning to Hawaii from Indonesia, Obama was enrolled at Punahou School. A recent article in *China Daily* pointed out that Punahou is the only school in the world where a future Chinese president, Sun Yat-Sen, and American president were educated.[18]

Obama does not mention what courses he took at Punahou, but it is likely that at a school in a majority–minority state where clocks give the time of developing nations and the curriculum is heavily weighted towards multiculturalism, he developed a keen knowledge of Hawaii's colonial past.[19] That past was bound up in the origins of Punahou itself. The school was founded by missionaries in 1841. The missionary movement would later play a crucial role in the overthrow of the Hawaiian monarchy in 1893.

In learning of his family's background, he developed an understanding of the legacy of British imperialism. On his visit to Nairobi, Kenya, as a senator in 2006, he told an audience at the local university that he learned of his ancestors while travelling in Kenya with his sister Auma on his first visit in 1987. He discovered that his grandfather was a highly respected elder in his village. However, working as a cook for the British, he suffered the humiliation of being called 'boy'.

Obama could tell his audience that his grandfather had been arrested during the infamous British military assault on Mau Mau rebels called Operation Anvil in 1954, which Catherine Elkins has characterized as 'the birth of Britain's Gulag', even though he was only 'at the periphery of Kenya's liberation struggles'.[20]

If his grandfather represented the colonial past, his father 'embodied the new Africa of the early Sixties, a man who had obtained the knowledge of the Western world, and sought to bring it back home, where he hoped he could create a new nation'.[21] In a speech during the campaign in Selma, Alabama, Obama made an attempt to link his father's destiny with the Civil Rights movement in the US. However, he erroneously claimed that the Kennedy family had had a hand in bringing his father to the US through an airlift aimed at bringing African students to the US and providing them with scholarships. The Kennedys did support such an airlift, but only after Barack Obama, Sr had come to Hawaii as a student. In reality, it was the efforts of a Kenyan, Tom Mboya, that made it possible for Obama's father to come to the US. Mboya, a labor leader and nationalist, came to the US in 1959 and 1960 to raise money for an airlift. He was able to secure funding from enough prominent donors active in the Civil Rights movement, such as the baseball player Jackie Robinson, the singer Harry Belafonte, and the actor Sidney Poitier, to bring eighty-one Kenyans, including Obama's father, to study in the US.[22]

However, Obama was right to point in the same speech to the connection between the Civil Rights movement and US foreign policy. During the Cold War, the US was regularly accused of hypocrisy in promoting freedom and democracy abroad while permitting segregation at home. As Mary Dudziak has argued, racist incidents such as lynchings and the brutal treatment of Civil Rights demonstrators sparked international outrage. One US Embassy official in Luanda, Angola explained that the arrest of Martin Luther King, Jr in Selma in 1965 damaged the image of the US in Angola and as a consequence, 'Africans can no longer trust US sympathetic statements re: African aspirations. They consider them hypocritical and devoid of any substance.'[23] Obama's sensitivity to the potential disconnect between US rhetoric and US actions have no doubt informed his views on foreign policy.

He was too young to be a part of the Civil Rights movement and Obama's first overt political activity was in the anti-apartheid movement that was fighting for divestment with South Africa at a time when the Reagan administration was preaching 'constructive engagement' as an alternative to sanctions against the South African government. At Occidental College, Obama was heavily involved in campus protests against the regime in South Africa. No doubt his late evening sessions with fellow students discussing the works of Fanon and the injustices of neocolonialism motivated his desire to protest against the apartheid regime in South Africa.

Unlike Kennedy, who spent considerable time in his twenties in Europe, or Reagan or Bush, who showed little interest in foreign travel before becoming president, Obama's curiosity about the world led him to travel to Pakistan in 1981. In speaking of the trip at a fundraiser during the campaign, Obama once again argued for the value of personal experience. As he put it, 'I knew what Sunni and Shia was before I joined the Senate Foreign Relations Committee.'[24]

Obama's understanding of the world was shaped by his experience as the son of a Kenyan immigrant to the US and an American from the heartland who spent most of her short life outside the US and gained a deep knowledge of foreign cultures. During his formative years, Obama's orientation was for the most part directed towards countries and regions that lay outside the East–West axis that informed the Cold War. As president, he inherits a world that has undergone marked geopolitical shifts since the end of the Cold War. Paradoxically enough, however, these changes have brought regions with which Obama is familiar to the forefront of the geopolitical nexus of the twenty-first century. A president with African roots, who spent a good part of his life in the Pacific region, has at least the potential to face the myriad challenges of a Post-American Century.

5
The Post-American Century

The short American Century

The history and future of American global power can be divided into two major phases with a brief interregnum. The short American Century lasted from the overthrow of Hawaii in 1893 to the fall of the Berlin Wall in 1989 that signalled the end of the Cold War. The second, triumphant, phase was intended as the start of the Next American Century, but it proved short lived. It lasted a mere twenty years, from the fall of the Berlin Wall in 1989 to the inauguration of Obama in 2009 which spelled the end of the Bush era. The next phase will likely be the Post-American Century. The US will for a time still be the most powerful nation on earth. However, it will have to share that power with a host of other rising powers, both state and non-state.

Two events, thousands of miles apart, set the stage for the American Century. Less than one hundred years before Obama came to Chicago, the city played host to an exposition that showcased the forward march of Western civilization. The World's Columbian Exposition was conceived to celebrate the 400th anniversary of Columbus's 'discovery' of America in 1492. Planning problems delayed its opening until 1893. It was here that a young historian, anxious to make an impression on the burgeoning historical profession, spoke at a special meeting of the American Historical Association about the significance of the frontier in American history. Frederick Jackson Turner noted that the Census of 1890 had declared that the frontier line no longer existed. Turner took the view that it was the encounter of European settlers with the American landscape that had forged the American character and explained American development.[25] Without the presence of the frontier, the American nation had entered a new phase.

Yet for the young historian, the growth of American cities was a cause for concern. Turner sought to make his mark in an increasingly professionalized field by offering a sweeping analysis of American progress, fully in keeping with the tone of the exposition, that placed the frontier experience as the epitome of the development of the American character. At the same time as he lauded the achievements of the American past, Turner was acutely aware that he was providing an epitaph to a soon-to-be-lost age. Indeed, the age of frontier hardiness, perserverance and perspicacity had already drawn to an end, according to the 1890 Census that Turner quoted at the very beginning of his talk. The note of apprehension he expressed about the future of the US in a land of no frontiers – his talk was entitled 'The Significance of the Frontier in American History' but could just as well have been called 'Whither the American Character?' – was belied by the setting of his talk. The exposition was an unabashed celebration of something larger than Turner's American frontier – the westward expansion of European empire of which the American expansion was an integral part.

The entire design of the exposition in Chicago was a paean to the virtues of European progress. Visitors could travel the world from the primitive outposts of Africa and Asia and end up at the White City, illuminated with countless electrical lights. Chicago was in the process of transforming itself into an urban frontier for the twentieth century that would produce an altogether different American character marked by social inequality and racial animosity. The celebration of 400 years of Euro-American expansion since Columbus 'discovered' the New World in 1492 willingly excluded or marginalized ethnic groups that were being subjected to colonial rule by European powers or that, in the US case, were regarded as second-class citizens.[26]

The exposition took place a mere nine years after the Berlin Conference in 1884 which effectively mandated the division of the African continent – including Barack Obama's ancestral home, Kenya – among leading European powers. The US, preoccupied with its continental expansion, had taken no part in these imperialist machinations. The 1890s would be different. The urge to emulate the European empires in their hunger for territory and spheres of influence proved irresistible.

An elderly African American came to the same exposition to deliver a different message. Frederick Douglass was invited to speak at a 'Colored American Day' event that the exposition's sponsors had hastily arranged to appease charges that they had been insensitive to African Americans. Another prominent figure in the African American community, Ida B. Wells, had urged a boycott of the event and published a pamphlet, *The Reason Why the Colored American is Not in the World's Columbian Exposition* which included an introduction by Douglass. As the US representative at the 'Haitian Pavillion', Douglass felt that it was important to make a public statement, so decided to accept the invitation.

In order to measure the extent of Western progress, the exposition set up pavilions of 'primitive' peoples from

Africa and Asia. Africa, the continent of Obama's ancestors, was represented by the 'Dahomey [now Benin] Pavillion'. At a time when the US could celebrate its progress as part of Western civilization and Turner could confer on Americans an identity linked to continental expansion, Africa was regarded as standing outside of history, truly a dark continent.

In his remarks, Douglass, instead of passively accepting the narrative the exposition was intended to convey, delivered a broadside against American hypocrisy:

> Men talk of the Negro problem. There is no Negro problem. The problem is whether the American people have loyalty enough, honor enough, patriotism enough, to live up to their own Constitution. We Negroes love our country. We fought for it. We ask only that we be treated as well as those who fought against it.[27]

Just before the Exposition in Chicago, events in the Pacific provided a perhaps unwitting resolution to the Turnerian dilemma of the future of the American character without the frontier. The starting point would be the islands where Barack Obama was born. Hawaii functioned as a proving ground for the continued western march of civilization heralded at the World's Columbian Exposition. In the early nineteenth century, American missionaries had come to what Captain James Cook had christened the Sandwich Island when he established the first European presence there in 1778. They were determined to bring the benefits of Christian civilization to what they regarded as heathen savages. Education was part of the civilizing mission. Obama's Punahou School was only one of many established by missionaries across the Hawaiian islands.

The missionaries soon realized that they and their families could become wealthy by exporting sugar from the islands, which entailed the expropriation of land from the native population for the construction of giant sugar plantations. Prevented by high tariffs imposed by the US from exporting sugar, the planter elite staged a coup against Queen Lili'uokalani, assisted by the US Marines. So began what Stephen Kinzer has called the century of regime change from Hawaii to Iraq.

Hawaii became an independent country under the control of the planter elite because President Benjamin Harrison, who supported annexation, was succeeded by Grover Cleveland, who opposed it. It was only five years after the overthrow that President William McKinley, in the midst of the Spanish–American War, decided to annex Hawaii to provide a staging post between California and the Philippines.[28]

The overthrow and subsequent annexation of Hawaii seemed to provide the solution to the future of the American character. If continental expansion would characterize the first phase of American development, overseas expansion would become its worthy successor.

In a long letter to President William McKinley in 1898, the Republican senator from Indiana, Albert Beveridge, remarked on the implications of the closing of the frontier that Turner had announced only five years earlier:

> How comes it that our first century closes with the process of consolidating the American people into a unit just accomplished, and quick upon the stroke of that great hour presses upon us our world opportunity, world duty, and world glory, which none but the people welded into an invisible nation can achieve or perform?[29]

In a speech before Congress in 1900, Beveridge made an impassioned plea in support of an American empire. After a century of 'self-government and internal development' the US should, in Beveridge's view, turn its attention to the 'administration and development of other lands'. His focus was the Pacific world. As an extension of the Spanish–American War in the Caribbean, the US had intervened in Spain's Pacific possession, the Philippines. Beveridge supported an American annexation of the Philippines, seeing it as part of a divine American mission to civilize primitive peoples. Expanding American power into the Pacific had another added benefit – China's 'illimitable markets'. The seas functioned as the highways of commerce, and since the Pacific was the ocean of future commerce and since most future wars would be 'conflicts for commerce', Beveridge reasoned, control of the Pacific would assure American world predominance.[30] Looking to the future, Beveridge later added, 'the twentieth century will be American. American thought will dominate it. American progress will give it color and direction. American deeds will make it illustrious.'[31]

Others shared Beveridge's optimism about an American Century. Brooks Adams envisioned the twentieth century as one of sustained American economic supremacy. Unlike Beveridge, Adams did not advocate outright colonialism in the name of a civilizing mission. He saw the Open Door policy towards China as a blueprint for US economic predominance based on preponderance of free trade. According to William Appleman Williams, this Open Door paradigm lay at the heart of US global expansionism in the twentieth century that he characterized as a form of imperial anticolonialism. Williams went so far as to claim that 'the history of the Open Door became the history of American foreign relations from 1900 to 1950'.[32] The British journalist William T. Stead joined in the chorus of those predicting that the twentieth century would indeed be the American Century. The title of his book summed up his argument: *The Americanization of the World, or The Trend of the Twentieth Century*. Stead regarded the US at the forefront of an Anglo-Saxon union that could regenerate the world.[33]

The Next American Century

On 9 November 1989 the Berlin Wall collapsed. Just a little over two years later, on Christmas Day 1991, the red flag with the hammer and sickle was lowered from the Kremlin. The Soviet Union was no more. Francis Fukuyama, an American and former policy adviser to President Ronald Reagan, saw in the new geopolitical order nothing less than the end of history. As he explained in an essay published in the summer of 1989 before the fall of the Wall,

> what we may be witnessing is not just the end of the Cold War, or the passing of a particular period of postwar history, but the end of history as such: that is, the end point of mankind's ideological evolution and the universalization of Western liberal democracy as the final form of human government.[34]

In the view of some conservatives, the end of history did not entail an American withdrawal from the world, however. Charles Krauthammer, a columnist for the *Washington Post*, published a long essay in *Foreign Affairs* that regarded the post-Cold War era as a unique opportunity for the US. The end of the Cold War's bipolar world and threat of nuclear annihilation did not herald the coming of a peaceful, multipolar world order, according to Krauthammer. Quite the contrary. For the foreseeable future, the US was the 'center of world power' in a 'new strategic enivironment' where the threat of conflict, far from diminishing, would increase. In a world with no other regional powers to challenge its predominance, the US should seize 'the unipolar moment'.[35]

President George H. W. Bush took a more benign view. In a speech delivered on 11 September 1990, Bush spoke of a 'new world order' in the context of the threat to world energy supplies posed by Iraq's occupation of

Kuwait. While emphasizing that there was no substitute for American leadership, Bush clearly regarded the new world order as one of cooperation with international institutions such as the United Nations and with allies across the world. The subsequent US-led military operation to expel Iraq from Kuwait in 1991 grew out of this vision.

Bush's reluctance to invade Iraq aroused concern among some of his advisers, however. The year after the Gulf War victory, the *New York Times* leaked a draft for the Defense Planning Guidance (DPG) that offered another, more muscular vision of a new world order in the post-Cold War world. The DPG is a Defense Department document, issued biannually, which describes American military strategy and is used as a basis for defense budgets. The first DPG after the demise of the Soviet Union was overseen by Paul Wolfowitz, Deputy Secretary of Defense and largely written by Zalmay Khalilzad, a member of his staff. The draft was more ambitious in scope than Krauthammer's 'unipolar moment'. Indeed, it expressed the view that this moment could be expanded to make the twenty-first century into yet another American Century. The most striking passages in the draft concern the long-term objectives of post-Cold War American military and political strategy. The primary objective was preventing any potential rival from attaining the power to dominate a particular region of the globe. In order to do so, the US had to demonstrate the required leadership to preclude the emergence of any rival powers. In 'non-defense areas' (presumably economic), the US should, moreover, take the interests of advanced industrial nations into account to discourage them from upsetting the 'established political and economic order'. Finally, and most importantly, the US should 'maintain the mechanisms for deterring potential competitors from even aspiring to a larger regional or global role'.[36]

This draft, disavowed and revised in 1992, proved to be the blueprint for the neoconservative foreign policy strategy that was formulated in opposition to the Clinton administration after Bush's defeat in 1992 and became an integral part of the geopolitical vision of Bush's son after 2001. The idea of US preponderance contributed to the start in 2003 of what neoconservative Michael Ledeen called 'the war to remake the world'.

Throughout the 1990s, the neoconservatives continued to articulate their vision of perpetual US predominance. Nowhere was this more evident than in the think tank Project for the Next American Century (PNAC).

Triumphalism infused the rhetoric of those neoconservatives who in the heady days of the 1990s imagined that the next century would simply continue the American dominance that had characterized the twentieth century. So much so, in fact, that one group decided to name their think tank Project for the Next American Century. Their statement of principles from 1997 would have done Beveridge proud. Reflecting an ill-concealed frustration with what they perceived as the vacillation and weakness of the Clinton administration, the signatories of the statement – who included conservative figures such as Jeb Bush, Dick Cheney, Francis Fukuyama, Zalmay Khalilzad, I. Lewis Libby, Norman Podhoretz, Donald Rumsfeld and Paul Wolfowitz – expressed their dismay at Clinton's 'incoherent policies' and yearned for 'the resolve to shape a new century favorable to American principles and interests'. They called for a return to a 'Reaganite policy of military strength and moral clarity', both of which they found singularly lacking in the Clinton administration.[37]

That return came with the foreign policy of George W. Bush.

In June 2002, President Bush delivered an address at West Point to the graduating cadets. His remarks drew on the neocon vision first expressed in the 1992 Defense Planning Guidance, elaborated by the PNAC in 1997 and elevated to the status of administration policy after the 9/11 attacks.

Bush's speech at West Point constituted a definitive break with the Cold War policy of deterrance and containment and its replacement by a policy of unilateral preemptive action by the US. It also shifted the focus of American foreign policy from stateless adversaries like the Al-Qaeda terrorist network to so-called rogue states like Iraq and weapons of mass destruction.

One of the most revealing statements to come out of the corridors of the Bush White House spoke volumes about how the Republicans in power viewed the world. Speaking to journalist Ron Suskind in 2004, an unnamed official laid bare the administration's tenuous grasp of agency in history. His reading of American foreign policy was the very essence of hubris – imagining oneself to be totally removed from social and historical constraints of any kind.

Suskind recounted how he didn't fully comprehend what the Bush senior adviser was saying at the time, but on reflection he felt that his statement got 'to the very heart of the Bush presidency'.

The aide said that guys like me were 'in what we call the reality-based community,' which he defined as people who 'believe that solutions emerge from your judicious study of discernible reality.' I nodded and murmured something about enlightenment principles and empiricism. He cut me off. 'That's not the way the world really works anymore,' he continued. 'We're an empire now, and when we act, we create our own reality. And while you're studying that reality – judiciously, as you will – we'll act again, creating other new realities, which you can study too, and that's how things will sort out. We're history's actors . . . and you, all of you, will be left to just study what we do.'[38]

It has, however, become increasingly clear that the US is not at the dawn of yet another American Century. Alongside the triumphalist neoconservative discourse – a discourse that intensified after the fall of the Berlin Wall and the collapse of the Soviet Union, and reached its zenith in the period immediately following 9/11 up to the invasion of Iraq – was a counterdiscourse that warned of the dangers of imperial overreach and called for the US to adapt to a new geopolitical order in which it would no longer enjoy absolute predominance.

Forty years before the neoconservative Defense Planning Guidance, the theologian Reinhold Niebuhr warned of the dangers of trying to supersede history. In *The Irony of American History*, he wrote of how

> a nation with an inordinate degree of political power is doubly tempted to exceed the bounds of historical possibilities, if it is informed by an idealism which does not understand the limits of man's wisdom and volition in history.[39]

As it happened, the 'unipolar moment' was short lived. It lasted about as long as another aberration from American foreign policy – the imperial moment that the McKinley administration kick-started with the Spanish–American War, a moment that ended with a whimper around 1914.

Rising powers

Obama takes office in a different world from the one envisioned by the DPG in the heady days after the fall of the Soviet Union. Far from being the Next American Century, the twenty-first century will in all likelihood be Post-American.

Two years before the fall of the Berlin Wall, a historian articulated an alternative vision for the US global role. In *The Rise and Fall of the Great Powers*, Paul Kennedy offered a trenchant analysis of the interplay between economic strength and military strategy over five centuries. It was, however, the final chapter of the book that attracted most attention. In his remarkably prescient conclusion, Kennedy looked to the future and argued that the US was in danger of succumbing to the same kind of 'imperial overstretch' – the failure to maintain a balance between wealth creation and military expenditure.[40] Kennedy's argument ran counter to the neoconservative notion that the US could in fact engage in countless military actions across the globe with impunity. Kennedy's viewpoint has been vindicated. In an op-ed written just before Obama's inaugural, he revisited his argument of more than twenty years ago:

> As I suggested at that time, a strong person, balanced and muscular, can carry an impressively heavy back-pack uphill for a long while. But if that person is losing strength (economic problems), and the weight of the burden remains heavy or even increases (the Bush doctrine), and the terrain becomes more difficult (rise of new Great Powers, international terrorism, failed states), then the once-strong hiker begins to slow and stumble. That is precisely when nimbler, less heavily burdened walkers get closer, draw abreast, and perhaps move ahead.[41]

In the same year that Bush articulated the Bush Doctrine, Charles Kupchan took up Kennedy's argument and predicted the imminent demise of the unipolar moment. In *The End of the American Era*, Kupchan implicitly warned of the dangers inherent in advocating a unilateral strategy in an age of profound geopolitical transformation. While acknowledging that the American era was 'alive and well' at the beginning of the twenty-first century, he believed that the rise of alternative centres of power was inevitable and that the US would do best in adjusting to this new geopolitical reality.

Pax Americana is poised to give way to a much more unpredictable and dangerous global environment. And the chief threat will come not from the likes of Osama bin Laden, but from the return of traditional geopolitical rivalry.

As a matter of urgency, America needs to begin to prepare itself and the rest of the world for this uncertain future. To wait until American dominance is already gone would be to squander the enormous opportunity that comes with primacy. America must devise a grand strategy for the transition to a world of multiple power centers now, while it still has the luxury of doing so. This is the central challenge of *The End of the American Era*.[42]

Kupchan may have been a lone voice in the months leading up to the invasion of Iraq, but the fiasco of that war (as one journalist, Thomas Ricks, has called it, notwithstanding the recent 'surge' of extra troops deployed to augment the US force in Iraq) and the financial crisis have called into question the strategy of unending US economic and military predominance. Joseph Stiglitz and Linda Bilmes have confirmed Kennedy's original warning against imperial overstretch by estimating the probable cost of the war in Iraq, which they calculated could be upwards of $3 trillion.[43]

A flurry of books and policy proposals have refuted the geopolitics of the Defense Planning Guidance–Bush Doctrine in favour of a recognition that the US should formulate a viable strategy that adapts to a world in which the US is one among many. It is this world that an Obama administration will confront.

Just after Obama was elected president, a report was released that described the world he was going to inherit. Every four years, the National Intelligence Council (NIC), which coordinates analysis from all US intelligence agencies, produces a global trends review. The study was designed to provide guidance for either sustaining or trying to prevent likely events in the future. The report released in 2008 looked ahead to 2025. In 2004, the year of Bush's re-election, the review comported well with the current mood in Washington and indeed with the kind of rhetoric emanating from the PNAC in the 1990s. Looking ahead to 2020, the 2004 review envisioned a world where the US was still the dominant power, with other powers having 'forsaken' the idea of posing any challenge to US predominance – essentially the realization of the DPG of 1992.

The 2008 assessment was considerably gloomier in its forecast. Far from seeing another American Century on the horizon, the review envisioned a world entering a Post-American Century. *Global Trends: 2025* foresees an international system unrecognizable from the one that emerged after World War II. In contrast to the previous report from 2004, which predicted 'continued US dominance', the new report foresees a transformed world in 2025 in which the US may well remain the single most powerful country but will be less dominant in an emerging new global multipolar system.[44]

Central to the assessment is the notion of the rise of a multipolar system, consisting of emerging powers and constituting a geopolitical power shift to the East. With the exception of Brazil, all the so-called BRIC nations (Brazil, Russia, India and China) are in the Asian hemisphere (Russia is often divided by the Urals into Europe and Asia). However, China emerges from the study as *primus inter pares*, predicted to have more 'impact on the world over the next twenty years than any other country'.[45]

In an implicit rebuke to the triumphalist discourse of the 'end of history' that was dominant during the 1989–91 period that witnessed the fall of the Berlin Wall and the dissolution of the Soviet Union, the NIC report stated that 'the western model of economic liberalism, democracy and secularism . . . which many assumed to be inevitable, may lose its luster – at least in the medium term'.[46]

In this new world, wealth would continue to move from west to east and state control of the economy 'may be gaining more appeal in the world' in the wake of the financial crisis. Furthermore, there is a danger that China's 'alternative economic model' may prove more attractive to developing nations, thus limiting the power of Western nations.[47] This trend could of course be exacerbated by the current financial crisis in the US, which has seriously damaged the reputation of the American model of capitalism.

There is increasing recognition that the world Obama will confront no longer conforms to the unipolar world of the immediate post-Cold War period. In retrospect, it would seem that Kupchan, writing in 2002 – a time when neoconservative ideas of American predominance were at their height – was prescient in predicting the end of the American era, rather than its continuation. While there is a difference in emphasis (or conceptualization) between observers of the geopolitics of the twenty-first century, all are agreed that the attempts to make the conflicts of the present conform to those of the immediate past were at best misguided.

If anything, the world that Obama confronts looks more like the pre-World War I world, with the increased risk of great power rivalries and a renewed scramble for scarce resources. The difference, of course, between the world of the so-called 'long peace' of 1815–1914 (during which European powers waged imperial wars in Africa and Asia) and the world of the twenty-first century is that while the former witnessed the rise of the West, the latter will likely consolidate the rise of the East.

The NIC does not stand alone. In 2008, there has been a veritable glut of studies seeking to make sense of a new world order in the twenty-first century. All are totally at odds with the Manichean world that formed the basis for American foreign policy during the Bush administration. Taken together, they both complement and supplement the analysis put forward by the NIC.

The neoconservative worldview gained strength in the 1990s as a strong oppositional force to the perceived weakness of the Clinton administration and it reached the apotheosis of its influence during the Bush administration. The neoconservative corpus spoke of the end of history and the US as the sole guarantor of stability in a Hobbesian world beset by violence. American liberals and Europeans in general were consigned to the dustbin of history.

Richard Haass, president of the Council of Foreign Relations, goes one step further than the NIC report and finds that the overriding characteristic of the twenty-first-century world resembles more chaos than order. While the twentieth century witnessed an increasing concentration of power, from the multipolar world of the early decades to the bipolar world of the Cold War and the unipolar moment of the post-Cold War era, the twenty-first century will be the age of nonpolarity that he defines as 'numerous centers with meaningful power'.[48] While Haass recognizes the geopolitical clout of the major powers – China, the EU, India, Japan, Russia and the US – he argues that the preeminence of these nation states is being 'challenged from above, by regional and global organizations; from below, by militias; and from the side, by a variety of nongovernmental organizations (NGOs) and corporations'.[49] In this new world, the US will remain 'the largest single aggregation of power' but that power is nevertheless subject to limits. Haass believes that the position of the US in the world is one of relative decline that will be accompanied by loss of influence and independence.

Fareed Zakaria agrees with Haass. During the campaign, Obama was photographed carrying Zakaria's *The Post-American World*, so he is at least familiar with its arguments. Zakaria makes it clear that by 'post-American' he does not mean that the US is no longer a dominant power. As he emphasizes in the opening sentence, 'This is a book not about the decline of America but rather about the rise of everyone else.'[50] These rising powers constitute the third tectonic shift of power since the age of Columbus. The first phrase witnessed the rise of the West, the second the dominance of the US, which lasted for most of the twentieth century and the beginning of the twenty-first century. Like Haass, Zakaria believes that American dominance, in virtually every dimension except political clout and military strength, is now being challenged by a host of different actors in different regions of the world.

Zakaria sees the potential for great power rivalries as China and India gain influence, as Russia becomes increasingly aggressive and as the European Union expands its sphere of influence. Pareg Khanna shares this concern. In *The Second World*, he describes a world in which three powers – China, the US and the EU – compete for access to energy and natural resources in countries in transition in Latin America, Central Asia, the Middle East and Asia. Each power approaches the world differently. Whereas the US still relies too heavily in employing military might to achieve its goals, the EU employs a more benign form of power – the opportunity for nations to become part of its sphere of influence. Mark Leonard takes this idea of European power a step further in *Why Europe Will Run the Twenty-first Century*, seeing it as a sign of strength. What Americans often perceive as weakness is, according to Leonard, an effective way of reshaping the world. China provides yet another model for augmenting its power. By pursuing a course of trade and investment in second world countries without any demands for reform or improvement of human rights, it can eclipse American power.[51]

The twenty-first-century world

In 2006 the Princeton Project on National Security, chaired by Anne Marie Slaughter and John Ikenberry, gathered a group of foreign policy analysts to chart a 'post-post 9/11 strategy'. Their conclusions in the final report stood in stark contrast to Bush administration policies.

They rejected the notion, touted by neoconservative Norman Podhoretz and coopted by Republican presidential candidate John McCain, that the US is engaged in a global struggle against Islamofascism – or World War IV as Podhoretz would have it – comparable to the wars against fascism and communism in the twentieth century. Indeed, the Princeton Project on National Security states emphatically that 'Americans need to recognize that ours is a world lacking a single organizing principle for foreign policy like anti-fascism and anti-communism'.[52]

In a slight to the overemphasis on military solutions to geopolitical problems advanced by the Bush administration, the Princeton Project outlines a strategy that resembles 'a Swiss Army knife' – a flexible foreign policy that offers different tools for different problems. Furthermore, the Project calls for a renewal of international institutions like the UN with active US participation. US foreign policy should be sensitive to the fact that 'others may perceive us differently than we perceive ourselves, no matter how good our intentions.'[53] The US should promote not only democracy, but a 'world of liberty under law' by working with international institutions. One of the PPNS proposals was, however, out of sync with the general tenor of the report. In an effort to strengthen solidarity between the world's democracies, the report suggested the establishment of a Concert of Democracies as a possible alternative to the UN if reforms are not implemented; and even, should the UN prove incapable of living up to its charter, a forum 'for the use of force'.[54]

This is the world Obama confronts at the beginning of the Post-American Century. Curiously, the global map of this new era bears some resemblance to that of what could be called the Pre-American Century, from the time of the founding of the US to the end of the nineteenth century.

142

Indeed, twenty-first-century politics has a sense of déjà vu about it.

Between 1808 and 1826, Latin America underwent a process of liberation from the Spanish Empire. During the American Century, however, the region was subject to multiple US interventions. A short respite came during the 1930s, when the Roosevelt administration announced its Good Neighbor policy, which entailed recognition of the sovereignty of Latin American and Caribbean nations and a pledge to stop military interventions. In *Empire's Workshop*, Greg Grandin argues that, just as US aggression in Latin America served as a laboratory for the development of new imperialism elsewhere, so the Good Neighbor policy became 'the model for the European and Asian alliance system'.[55]

In the spring of 2001, at a Summit of the Americas held in Canada in Quebec City, President George W. Bush laid out his vision of 'a fully democratic hemisphere bound together by goodwill and free trade' for the new century. He concluded his remarks by urging the delegates to use the summit 'to launch the century of the Americas'.[56] The century of the Americas did not materialize. On the contrary, developments in the twenty-first century regarding trade issues and policies pursued by left-leaning governments (in especially Venezuela, Bolivia and Ecuador) have drawn the US and Latin America further and further apart.

During his election campaign, Obama expressed a willingness to negotiate with Venezuela's leader Hugo Chavez, whom the Bush administration regarded as little more than a pariah. Moreover, Obama has spoken of pursuing a normalization of relations with Cuba.

He issued a policy statement, 'A New Partnership for the Americas,' which contained wide-ranging proposals for improving relations with the entire region. Some of the suggestions concerning trade agreements were clearly motivated by campaign considerations. Yet Obama made a point of referring to FDR's Four Freedoms as essential components of US policy in the Americas, an indication that he intended to draw on the example of the Roosevelt administration. No doubt inspired by the example of his mother, Obama's section on 'freedom from want' proposes focusing on microfinance as one way of alleviating poverty. A revival of the Good Neighbor policy towards Latin America could well constitute a template for US foreign policy in other regions of the world.[57]

The Open Door Policy with China that influenced much of American foreign policy in the twentieth century has been transformed into another symbiotic relationship, which the historian Niall Ferguson has dubbed Chimerica, the fusion of the two nations that has accounted for more than half of economic growth in the twenty-first century. The relationship between the two nations is, in Ferguson's view, 'the most important thing to understand about the world economy in the last ten years'. The financial crisis will accelerate the 'great reconvergence' between East and West, with China predicted to overtake the US in gross domestic product as early as 2027.[58]

The relationship between the US and China also has a military dimension. The Pacific Command (PACOM), with its headquarters in Obama's birthplace Hawaii, had a vested interest in containing Chinese power projection in the Pacific. The Chinese government, however, determined to secure a first-world lifestyle for its citizens, has built submarines to open sea lanes for the unobstructed transport of vital energy supplies. Just over 100 years after the Open Door policy, with Hawaii as part of a range of stepping stones in the Pacific archipelago designed to secure US economic and military predominance, the rise of China has changed the balance of power in the area. As Robert Kaplan put it, 'America's complete dominance over the Pacific was over. China seemed determined to be the master of subtle, peaceful influence, something that, after all, required a military component. It was a reality with which we had to come to terms.'[59]

The fact that the Obama administration chose to send Secretary of State Hillary Clinton to Asia on her first trip abroad – and that before she left for Asia she noted the US was a transpacific as well as a transatlantic nation – spoke volumes about how it viewed the geopolitical balance of power. However, the Obama administration will have to accommodate itself to a China that is determined to be a global power.

At her confirmation hearings, Clinton spoke of the need to employ 'smart power' in future US foreign relations. This term was first used by Suzanne Nossel, a former official at the UN, in an essay in *Foreign Affairs* in 2004. Nossel argued for a revival of the liberal internationalism of the Roosevelt era, lamenting that conservatives had appropriated its rhetoric but not its content. She noted that the US, the sole superpower after World War II, had willingly entered into alliances and contributed to the founding of the UN and NATO. In her view,

> progressives, therefore, must reframe U.S. foreign policy according to their abiding belief that an ambitious agenda to advance freedom, trade, and human rights is the best long-term guarantee of the United States' security against terrorism and other threats.[60]

Clinton, however, sent mixed messages during her trip to Asia. She was criticized by human rights organizations for sidelining human rights issues with the Chinese in favour of issues like climate change and the financial crisis. In Indonesia on the other hand, she noted the transformation that had taken place since the deposition of Suharto, who had been in power since Obama lived there as a boy, up until the 1998 Asian financial crisis. In a clear indication that Indonesia is likely to play a significant role in US Asia policy, Clinton complimented her hosts: 'If you want to know if Islam, democracy, modernity and women's rights can coexist, go to Indonesia.'[61]

In the nineteenth century, the British and Russian Empire engaged in an ongoing rivalry to achieve imperial control of Central Asia. In the Post-American Century, Obama may have to contend with a New Great Game to dominate the region surrounding the Caspian Sea, a rich source of natural gas. Players in the region include China, Russia and Iran as well as non-state actors such as transnational energy corporations. A resurgent Russia has also given rise to the prospect of a new Cold War, especially with the prospect of possible NATO expansion into Ukraine and Georgia. As with the Pacific region, there is a military component to the balance of power in the region. The Shanghai Cooperation Organization (SCO), consisting of China, Russia and four former Soviet republics – Kazakhstan, Kyrgyzstan, Tajikistan and Uzbekistan – was established in 2001 and deals primarily with trade, counterterrorism and drug trafficking, although it has also conducted joint military exercises. Some military analysts believe that the SCO is intent on preventing US access to the region's energy resources.[62] Just weeks after Obama took office, the government of Kyrgyzstan announced that it would close the US air base at Manas which the military was using for incursions into Afghanistan. Loss of the air base would seriously impair Obama's plans to escalate the war in Afghanistan. The decision came shortly after Russian President Dmitri Medvedev had offered poverty-stricken Kyrgyzstan a substantial loan to cover the country's debts. The motivation for such largesse was not hard to discern – Russia had long objected to what it saw as an intrusion into the Russian sphere of influence in the region.

In the Middle East, Obama will face the nation many have called the real winner of the war in Iraq – Iran. Obama's pledge to negotiate with Iran would constitute a virtual about-face in US policy in the region. The Bush administration envisioned a free and democratic Iraq having a domino effect and resolving the Israel–Palestine conflict through the back door. Improved relations with Iran, which exerts considerable influence with Syria, as well as Hizbollah in Lebanon and Hamas in Gaza, could in the long term accelerate the peace process between Israel and Palestine. In a speech at the American Israel Public Affairs Committee (AIPAC), Obama laid out his plans for peace in the Middle East, which included conducting strong diplomacy with Iran as well as showing a commitment to the Israeli–Palestinian peace process early on in his presidency.[63] One week after his inauguration, Obama sent his special envoy to the Middle East, George Mitchell, to the region.

Obama ran on a pledge to withdraw from Iraq. However, the situation there is far from stable and an end to the war may be a long time in coming. Drawing on extensive talks with many who have served in Iraq, *Washington Post* journalist Thomas Ricks ends his book *The Gamble* with the prediction that the US may only be half way through the war, meaning that an American presence will likely be maintained until at least 2015, way past the deadline stipulated by the Status-of-Forces Agreement (SOFA) signed by the Bush administration and the Iraqi government.[64] Winning the 'right' war in Afghanistan may also prove to be increasingly difficult in light of the growing strength of the Taliban and the corruption of the Hamid Karzai government and its limited capacity to control the country.

Undaunted by these potential problems, Obama gave a major speech on Iraq at Camp Lejeune in North Carolina. Bush had come to Camp Lejeune in April 2003 to speak to the troops about achieving final victory in Iraq. Obama came almost six years later to announce the beginning of the end of the war. He set a date for US withdrawal of 31 August 2010. However, the US presence in Iraq would not end on that date. A residual force, which would 'likely be made up of 35–50,000 troops', would remain to help the Iraqi government and to protect 'our ongoing civilian and military efforts' until the SOFA deadline.[65]

The Obama administration's commitment to finding lasting solutions to conflict in the entire Middle East and Central Asia was demonstrated by the decision to appoint three high-level envoys to those unstable regions – George Mitchell, Richard Holbrooke to coordinate US policy towards Afghanistan and Pakistan, and Dennis Ross to deal with Iran policy. However, Obama's decision to shift the focus of US military operations from Iraq to Afghanistan–Pakistan, where the long war began in October 2001, may prove counterproductive. Even with the expected deployment of an additional 30,000 troops, as Obama has proposed, the combined NATO and Afghan forces fighting the Taliban would reach 200,000, a third of the troop numbers in Iraq. Along with Iraq, Afghanistan and Pakistan are failed states and it is far from certain that the deployment of more American troops in Afghanistan will help in establishing a cohesive state there.[66]

The Scramble for Africa in the late nineteenth century carved up the continent between the great European powers of the day in a relentless drive for material resources and slaves. The New Scramble for Africa is also about resources, particularly oil in countries like Nigeria and Angola, with new powers like China, India, Malaysia and Russia vying with the US for access to vital resources. The US already relies on Africa for about 20 per cent of its imported oil, primarily from Nigeria, Angola and Equatorial Guinea, with that figure expected to rise to 25 per cent by 2015. In 2002 the Assistant Secretary of State for African Affairs, Walter Kansteiner, declared that 'African oil is of strategic national interest to us' and 'it will increase and become more important as we go forward'. Like China in the Pacific, the US military under the European Command has conducted

exercises off the West coast of Africa to secure sea lanes con-
necting offshore oil platforms with the eastern US.[67]
Evidence of the increasing importance of Africa to US
foreign and national security policy came in 2007 with the
announcement from the Bush administration of the forma-
tion of the US Africa Command (AFRICOM). Previously,
Africa had been the area of responsibility of three com-
mands. Even though the Command's website cites its main
task as war prevention, the strategic importance of African
oil has no doubt played a role in the creation of AFRICOM.[68]
Whether the Obama administration will change course
and use AFRICOM to fight wars against genocide and to
provide protection for aid workers fighting disease remains
to be seen. There is also a danger that the US military presence on this continent might lead to involvement in the
longest running war in recent times – the so-called Congo
Wars, a conflict that has claimed, by conservative estimate,
over three million lives.[69]

The US abolished the slave trade in 1807, but maintained the institution of slavery until after the Civil War.
On their trips to Africa, Presidents Clinton and George
W. Bush stopped short of offering an official apology to
African nations for the US role in the slave trade. Perhaps
a President Obama, of African descent with a wife whose
ancestors were slaves, might deliver just such an apology.

Up until 1949, the US had no permanent alliances with
European nations, heeding George Washington's warning
from 1796 against 'interweaving our destiny with that of
any part of Europe' as he questioned the benefits of entan-
gling 'our peace and prosperity in the toils of European
ambition, rivalship, interest, humor or caprice'.[70] In 1949,
the US entered into the first peacetime military alliance
outside of the Western Hemisphere when it signed the
treaty establishing NATO. In his Berlin speech, Obama
made it clear that he expected NATO to contribute more
troops in Afghanistan, a message that received mixed

reaction in Europe. Obama has paid lip service to maintaining close ties with Europe, but differences over the role of NATO in the twenty-first century could lead to tensions between the Obama administration and European NATO members. Proposals for NATO expansion into Ukraine and Georgia have already caused tensions between the alliance and Russia, which objects to the presence of a Western alliance in former republics of the Soviet Union.

The American Century started in Cuba and in the Pacific, with the annexation of two island nations, Hawaii and the Philippines, and the Open Door policy towards China. The Post-American Century will be marked by a shift from West to East and the imminent rise of China as the next global superpower. Obama, with roots in the Pacific, will preside over a US that is no longer the single dominant economic, military or cultural force in the world.

6

The Obama Doctrine

A 'dumb' war

Obama may have burst on the national stage with his speech at the Democratic National Convention in 2004, but the initial success of his candidacy for president owed a good deal to a speech he gave in October 2002, when he was a relatively unknown state senator from Illinois.

During the general election campaign in 2008, Republican vice-presidential candidate Sarah Palin became the object of much ridicule in the press after she, in an interview with ABC anchor Charles Gibson, was at a loss to define the Bush Doctrine. In June 2002 President George W. Bush gave the commencement speech at the US military academy at West Point. It was there that he arguably articulated the clearest formulation of the Bush Doctrine. He declared that 'the war on terror will not be won on the defensive. We must take the battle to the enemy, disrupt his plans, and confront the worst threats before they emerge. In the world we have entered, the only path to safety is the path of action. And this nation will act.'[71]

The West Point speech was significant because it signalled the beginning of a concerted campaign to mobilize public opinion behind an invasion of Iraq. In October, the Bush administration stepped up its rhetoric and put forward a resolution before Congress authorizing the president to use military force against the regime of Saddam Hussein in Iraq.

As a reaction to the proposed resolution, an anti-war group in Chicago organized a demonstration on 2 October. They invited Obama, then a state senator representing the South Side of Chicago, to speak at the rally.

Obama began by making it clear that he did not oppose all wars. He spoke of the valiant cause of the Civil War and of his grandfather's service in World War II. He did, however, oppose what he called 'dumb' and 'rash' wars, like the one that the administration's 'armchair' warriors intended to wage as part of their 'ideological agenda'. He regarded the impending war in Iraq as a politically motivated war designed to distract the attention of the American people from pressing problems at home – social inequality and a looming economic depression. Reiterating the phrase 'You want a fight, President Bush', Obama then listed causes he felt were worth fighting for: stopping Osama bin Laden and Al-Qaeda, enforcing non-proliferation treaties, preventing 'so-called' allies in the Middle East from oppressing their people, and working to gain energy independence from Middle East oil.[72]

At the time, Bush still enjoyed high approval ratings. A number of Democratic senators, some with their eyes on the White House, supported Bush's resolution. All of Obama's rivals for the Democratic nomination who were members of Congress at the time (with the exception of Dennis Kucinich) voted for the resolution.

Obama's speech received little attention at the time. During the period of the build-up to the war, public opinion had been shaped by administration assurances that the regime of Saddam Hussein constituted an imminent threat to the national security of the US. Top administration officials warned that failure to stop Saddam could result in 'a mushroom cloud'.

Bush went to war on 19 March 2003. During the first phase of the war, which lasted until Bush announced on 1 May 2003 that 'major combat operations' were over, public approval of the war was high. During the Reconstruction period, however, the death toll for American troops mounted. Revelations that Saddam did not possess weapons of mass destruction, and news of the torture of Iraqi prisoners at Abu Ghraib, contributed to growing public opposition to the war.

By the time of the mid-term elections of 2006, the War in Iraq had lasted longer than the American engagement in World War I and was fast approaching the length of American engagement in World War II. Public dissatisfaction with the war was cited as one of the main reasons that voters turned to the Democrats and gave them control of both houses of Congress. The war had proved an albatross, not only for George W. Bush, but also for those Democrats who had supported him in 2002. In late 2006, Obama's characterization of the war as 'dumb' looked more prescient than misguided.

In the course of 2007 a number of candidates announced that they were seeking the Democratic nomination. Polls showed that many Americans viewed the War in Iraq as one of the most important issues for the forthcoming election in 2008. Obama used his early opposition to the war to his advantage during the primary campaign. The two other frontrunners, Hillary Clinton and John Edwards, were forced to explain why they had voted as they had in 2002. Edwards expressed regret; Clinton never entirely disavowed her decision to support Bush. When Clinton accused Obama of not having the requisite experience to be commander in chief, Obama countered that he had shown the kind of judgement befitting a president on 'the single most important foreign policy decision since the end of the Cold War'.

In a revealing exchange during one of the Democratic presidential candidates' debates in late January 2008, Obama went beyond just stating his opposition to the war.

'I don't want to just end the war,' he declared emphatically, 'but I want to end the mind-set that got us into war in the first place.' Asked what Obama meant by changing the mind-set, several of Obama's foreign policy advisers emphasized the concept of 'dignity promotion', i.e. improving social and economic conditions so that democracy and the rule of law can develop.[73]

Obama insisted that he wanted to end the war in Iraq as soon as possible. He put forward a plan to withdraw from Iraq in 18 months, leaving only a small residual force. However, especially during the general election campaign, he was forced to counter John McCain's accusation that he had come out against Bush's escalation of troops in Iraq – the 'surge' that McCain had been calling for since the beginning of the war. Since the surge (which began in 2007 with the deployment of extra troops to augment the US fighting force) seemed to be working, Obama was forced in an interview to admit that it had in fact reduced violence in Iraq.

For his part, though, McCain insisted that the War in Iraq would be fought until final victory, something the majority of the American people were loathe to hear. His statements about the need to combat Islamofascism until final victory was achieved derived from the writings of one of his top foreign policy advisers, the neoconservative Norman Podhoretz, who had expressed such belligerent views in his book *World War IV*.

The economic crisis preoccupied voters in the weeks leading up to the election. However, public fatigue with the war, coupled with the financial crisis, which many voters associated with the party in power, clearly helped Obama in the general election.

One world

Obama came to Berlin in July 2008. His campaign had arranged for him to give a speech in the once-divided city, where John F. Kennedy in 1963 and Ronald Reagan in 1987 gave memorable speeches with the Berlin Wall as a backdrop. The inevitable comparisons between presidential candidate Obama's speech and those of two US presidents were of course not lost on the candidate himself and his advisers. Unlike JFK and Reagan, Obama was not the president of the US, merely the 'presumptive' nominee of the Democratic Party. JFK spoke less than a year after the Cuban missile crisis when the world seemed on the brink of nuclear conflagration. Reagan was speaking at a time of great flux on the European continent. The new Soviet leader Mikhail Gorbachev had, after his ascension to the post of Communist Party General Secretary in 1985, initiated sweeping reforms of the Soviet system. Just over two years after Reagan urged Gorbachev to tear down the Berlin Wall, jubilant crowds in East Berlin proceeded to do just that. JFK and Reagan employed rhetoric befitting a bifurcated world split between East and West that had essentially been in place since 1946, a fact noted by Britain's Winston Churchill in his famous 'iron curtain' speech in Independence, Missouri.

Three years prior to Churchill's speech, in the middle of the Second World War, a book was published offering another vision of the postwar world. The Republican presidential candidate who had been defeated by FDR in 1940, Wendell Willkie, published a travelogue of a forty-nine-day trip around the globe which he entitled, simply, *One World*. It became a runaway bestseller and by the end of 1944, when it was clear that the Axis Powers would lose the war, Willkie's book had been translated into many languages and had sold an unprecedented 4.5 million copies.[74] Willkie spoke of a new 'small and completely interdependent' world in the face of the virulent nationalisms of German and Italian fascism, facilitated by the relative ease of air travel which had obliterated the distance between nations. The future, Willkie declared, should be marked by 'worldwide' thinking.[75]

No doubt the popularity of Willkie's book reflected a good portion of wishful thinking on the part of its readers; a yearning for a united, interdependent world after the cataclysmic events of the previous five years. However, as David Reynolds observes in his global history of the postwar era – entitled, pointedly, *One World Divisible* – Willkie's world may well have been shrinking in terms of 'interconnectedness in travel and trade, ideas and information' but it was at the same time beset by seemingly insurmountable divisions. As Reynolds puts it, 'the striking feature of recent decades has been the dialectical process of greater integration *and* fragmentation.'[76]

Obama was of course mindful of the JFK and Reagan speeches and employed the image of walls coming down as a tribute. However, the title of his address, 'A World Shared As One', bore more resemblance to Willkie's idea of an integrated, interconnected world. He told his enthusiastic audience that he had come to Berlin not only as an American, but as a citizen of the world. Echoing JFKs phrase, 'let them come to Berlin,' Obama encouraged the people of the world to 'look at Berlin' as an example of a future united world.

Obama took issue with prevailing wisdom in Europe that the US 'is part of what has gone wrong in our world' and Americans who wilfully 'deride and deny the importance of Europe's role'. In an intertwined world, 'the burdens of global citizenship continue to bind us together'. Partnership and cooperation should form the basis for transatlantic relations in the twenty-first century.

Obama implicitly evoked the importance of dignity promotion. Recognizing that globalization had left many behind, he used the example of the Berlin airlift in 1948 to call for a renewed effort to help those in need:

> Will we extend our hand to the people in the forgotten corners of this world who yearn for lives marked by dignity and opportunity; by security and justice? Will we lift the

child in Bangladesh from poverty, shelter the refugee in Chad, and banish the scourge of AIDS in our time? Will we stand for the human rights of the dissident in Burma, the blogger in Iran, or the voter in Zimbabwe? Will we give meaning to the words 'never again' in Darfur?[77]

He spoke of the need to welcome immigrants and used the image of the US, where 'every language is spoken' and 'every culture has left its imprint', to evoke the Four Freedoms of Franklin D. Roosevelt (though without mentioning his name) – of speech, of religion, from want and from fear – as a uniting ideal for all mankind.

In *A New Deal for the World*, Elizabeth Borgwardt argues that it was just such an organizing principle based on the Four Freedoms, established just after World War II, that contributed to a new world order based on human rights.[78] According to Joseph Nye, FDR's Four Freedoms proved a powerful example of what he defines as 'soft' power, i.e. the ability to obtain results through the attraction of American ideals and culture, instead of by coercion.[79]

Of course, such notions of US benevolence can easily be used to defend the idea of the exceptional role of the US in the world that can be counterproductive. Obama succumbed to the rhetoric of the US as the 'last, best hope on earth' in a number of his foreign policy statements. The question for the future of the Obama Doctrine is whether he will be able to go beyond it. Arguably, his experience living outside the US, and the ties he has with family living on all continents, have contributed to a recognition that the US often acts in its own self-interest and not just for the benefit of the world community. His discussion of US foreign policy in *The Audacity of Hope* is a case in point. Looking at Indonesia, which he says provides 'a handy record of U.S. foreign policy over the past fifty years', he acknowledges that the US record there – and across the globe – has been mixed.

In broad outline at least, it's all there: our role in liberating former colonies and creating international institutions to help manage the post-World War II order; our tendency to view nations and conflicts through the prism of the Cold War; our tireless promotion of American-style capitalism and multinational corporations; the tolerance and occasional encouragement of tyranny, corruption, and environmental degradation when it served our interests; our optimism once the Cold War ended that Big Macs and the Internet would lead to the end of historical conflicts; the growing economic power of Asia and the growing resentment of the United States as the world's sole superpower; the realization that in the short term, at least, democratization might lay bare, rather than alleviate, ethnic hatreds and religious divisions – and that the wonders of globalization might also facilitate economic volatility, the spread of pandemics, and terrorism.[80]

This litany with respect to the US role in the world is a far cry from the complacent American exceptionalism that dominates foreign policy discussions. In his public statements, Obama has trodden the line of American exceptionalism while in subtle ways he has tried to undermine it. His own background has no doubt contributed to this skepticism about the US global role.

Towards an Obama Doctrine

It is perhaps premature to speak of an Obama Doctrine at this early stage in his presidency. Looking at his foreign policy advisers, however, may provide insight into the kind of policies Obama intends to pursue in the Post-American Century.

Think tanks have come to play an important role in the formulation of presidential foreign policy. Ronald Reagan relied on the conservative Heritage Foundation. Bill Clinton sought counsel from the more progressive Brookings Institution. The conservative American Enterprise Institute had close ties with the Bush administration. The Center for a New American Security (CNAS) was founded in February 2007 by Kurt Campbell and Michele Flournoy, two former Clinton administration officials. John Podesta, former Clinton chief of staff, who headed Obama's transition, serves on the CNAS board of directors. It is expected that Obama will draw on the CNAS for advice on policy and that some of its members will take on mid-level foreign policy positions in the Obama administration.[81] Shortly after Obama took office, Flournoy was appointed Undersecretary of Defense for Policy.

A primary focus of CNAS is counterinsurgency. Two of the most prominent thinkers at CNAS are John Nagl and Nathaniel Fick. Nagl, a retired US Army officer, led a tank battalion task force in Iraq and was one of the co-authors of the Army's new *Counterinsurgency Field Manual*. Fick's marine platoon in Iraq was the subject of Evan Wright's *Generation Kill* which was later made into an HBO series.

In an article in *Foreign Policy*, Nagl and Fick summed up the counterinsurgency strategy:

> To avoid repeating the mistakes of the Vietnam War, the U.S. military would have to relearn and institutionalize that conflict's key lessons. At the time, the doctrine the manual laid out was enormously controversial, both inside and outside the Pentagon. It remains so today. Its key tenets are simple, but radical: Focus on protecting civilians over killing the enemy. Assume greater risk. Use minimum, not maximum force.[82]

David Kilcullen, an Australian lieutenant colonel and anthropologist currently working as a fellow for the CNAS, has been instrumental in formulating how these strategies can be used in the twenty-first century. He is careful to take into account the globalization effects that have transformed the nature of insurgency since the war in Vietnam. The new insurgency is transnational.[83] At the request of then Deputy Secretary of Defense Paul Wolfowitz, Kilcullen contributed the section on irregular warfare in the Pentagon's Quadrennial Defense Review. He characterized the current conflict as a 'long war' and proposed that US forces attain 'greater language skills and cultural awareness'. A caption on a photograph in the report showing US soldiers at a police recruiting station in Iraq reads, 'The U.S. Army is harnessing the diversity of American society by recruiting heritage speakers of priority languages to serve as translators and interpreters.'[84]

The Counterinsurgency Field Manual (2007) reflects Kilcullen's views. In the section on intelligence in counterinsurgency, the *Manual* proposes that intelligence gathering take into account the social structure, culture and languages of host societies.[85] These efforts are a clear attempt by the US military and intelligence establishments to counter the cultural myopia and excessive reliance on military solutions to political problems that have plagued US foreign policy in the past.

Kilcullen advised General David Petraeus on counterinsurgency tactics during the early days of the surge in Iraq. As a senior fellow at the CNAS, Kilcullen is now working closely with the Obama administration to help formulate policy on Afghanistan and Pakistan, helping write two reviews that Obama has read. He has been critical of what he calls the 'enemy-centric' approach of the US military in Afghanistan, which focuses on hunting down the Taliban instead of protecting the local populace. Kilcullen believes this approach is counterproductive in the long run. He points out that the majority of those regarded as Taliban are fighting for local or nationalistic reasons and would be open to negotiation. Kilcullen advocates deploying US military in the local communities. Living among the local populace enables the military to provide assistance and build trust over time.[86]

The Pakistani journalist Ahmed Rashid expands on this kind of thinking. In *Descent into Chaos*, he mounts a blistering critique on the failed policies of the Bush administration, which have, in his view, left 'a far more unstable world' seven years after the 9/11 attacks. 'Ultimately the strategies of the Bush administration have created a far bigger crisis in South and Central Asia than existed before 9/11,' he writes, and he proposes 'a new global compact' in the region to help with its myriad problems, ranging 'from settling the Kashmir dispute between India and Pakistan to funding a massive education and job-creation programme in the borderlands between Afghanistan and Pakistan and along their borders with Central Asia'.[87] That Rashid has Obama's ear is indisputable. In January, he flew in from Lahore, Pakistan to attend a meeting with Obama at the Woodrow Wilson International Center for Scholars and, among others, Obama advisers Samantha Power and Scott Gration, Wilson Center president Lee Hamilton (one of the co-authors of the Iraq Study Group report) and Indian-born Pepsi CEO Indra Nooyi.[88]

Much of the focus on the Obama administration's foreign policy has understandably been on his top-level appointees. His main rival for the Democratic presidential nomination, Hillary Clinton, was appointed as Secretary of State. In an expected move, Robert Gates, Secretary of Defense in the Bush administration, was asked to stay on. James Jones, who had worked for the Bush administration as special envoy for Middle East security, was named as National Security Adviser. Janet Napolitano, the governor of Arizona, was tapped as the third Secretary of Homeland Security. One of Obama's closest advisers, Susan Rice, who many speculated was in line for Secretary of State, was made Ambassador to the United Nations. Obama reinstated the UN Ambassador as a full cabinet post, as it had been under the Clinton administration.

Rice had been Undersecretary of State for African Affairs during the Clinton administration, but threw her support behind Obama early on in the primaries. As a Senior Fellow at the Brookings Institution, Rice had focused on Africa, failed states, development issues and multilateral diplomacy. Seeing the horrific results of the warfare in Rwanda on a visit in 1994, she became a vocal critic of the Bush administration's inaction over seeking to stop the genocide in Darfur. Obama visited a refugee camp in Chad on his trip to Africa in 2006 and sponsored the Menendez Amendment for UN peacekeeping in Darfur. One of the first tests for his new administration will be how to react to the warrant issued by the International Criminal Court for the arrest of Omar al-Bashir, the president of Sudan.

Genocide in Africa is also a prime concern for another Obama adviser, Samantha Power, Professor at the Carr Center for Human Rights Policy in the Kennedy School of Government at Harvard. Obama had read her Pulitzer Prize-winning book on US foreign policy and genocide, *A Problem from Hell*, over Christmas in 2004 and requested a meeting in 2005. In her book, Power was openly critical of the Clinton administration's failure to act in the face of the Rwandan genocide.[89]

She became a top foreign policy adviser to the Obama campaign but was forced to resign after she, thinking she was speaking off the record, told a Scottish journalist that Hillary Clinton was a 'monster' for the way she was running her campaign. She returned as part of Obama's transition team after the election and was named senior director for multilateral affairs at the National Security Council.

On a stop in California promoting her latest book (a biography of the UN special envoy to Iraq, Sergio Vieira de Mello, who was killed when a bomb blew up UN headquarters in Baghdad in 2003), Power spoke passionately of de Mello's belief in talking to dictators, in 'dignity promotion', i.e. meeting basic material needs as a prerequisite for real democratic development, and in creating the conditions for a freedom from want and from fear. Power recalled that a 'number of people came up to me afterwards and said, "Wow, that's the Obama Doctrine," and I was like, "Oh my god, it is."'[90]

The end of American exceptionalism

July 2009 marks the thirtieth anniversary of one of the most remarkable speeches given by an American president. In the summer of 1979, President Jimmy Carter announced to the nation that he would soon give a major policy speech on energy. He retreated to Camp David and for ten days listened to consultations with Americans from all walks of life. On 15 July 1979 he delivered a speech that touched on the energy crisis, but focused on what Carter regarded as a larger problem – the crisis of confidence that had sapped the energy of the American people. Carter's address to the nation was later dubbed the 'malaise' speech, although he never used the word. However, the description was apt, because Carter pointed to a general 'crisis of confidence' that threatened 'to destroy the social and political fabric of America'. Not only were Americans losing confidence in the future, they were turning away from the past, living in a present that focused on self-indulgence and consumption. American national identity is 'no longer defined by what one does, but by what one owns', Carter announced.

The immediate solution to this crisis, according to Carter, would be to impose limits on energy consumption. He was emphatic on the need to wean the US from dependence on foreign oil: 'Beginning this moment, this nation will never use more foreign oil than we did in 1977 – never.'[91]

Three momentous events had preceded Carter's presidency and had in a sense set the stage for the malaise speech. In 1973, the Organization of Petroleum Exporting Countries (OPEC) had declared an oil embargo in response to US support for Israel during the Yom Kippur war. One year later, President Nixon had resigned in disgrace as a result of the Watergate scandal. Less than a year after Nixon's ignominious resignation, the US had suffered its first military defeat in Vietnam. Carter won the presidency in 1976 as a direct result of a national disillusionment with government and a desire for change.

In foreign policy, Carter attempted to move the country beyond the Vietnam debacle by rejecting the Cold War thinking that had made the US see all global conflict through the prism of the conflict between the US and the Soviet Union. In June 1977, Carter delivered a major foreign policy address at Notre Dame University. 'Human Rights and Foreign Policy' was an attempt to reconcile foreign policy with the American national character. All too often, Carter proclaimed, the US was willing to compromise its principles in the name of political expediency. Vietnam was a prime example of this wayward course. To that end, he expressed his firm belief that the US had now moved beyond the 'inordinate fear of Communism' that had compromised American values. Carter wanted to make the fight for human rights the cornerstone of American foreign policy. Furthermore, he proposed that the US devote its resources to combating 'hunger, disease, illiteracy, and repression' and called for closer cooperation between the US and 'newly influential countries in Latin America, Africa, and Asia'.[92]

When Carter took office in 1977, two opposing views of the future of American foreign policy had emerged in the wake of the failure of detente. The Committee for the Present Danger (CPD), formed in 1950 to lobby for the military build-up proposed by National Security Council Report 68, was revived in 1976 as an outgrowth of Team B, which President Gerald Ford had established to assess whether the CIA had underestimated Soviet capabilities. Team B released a report warning that the Soviet Union was seeking global hegemony and the reconstituted CPD lobbied for a massive defence build-up in order to ensure continued US military superiority. Team B and the CPD were in effect a precursor to the Project for the Next American Century (PNAC). One of Team B's members, Paul Wolfowitz, was one of the founders of the PNAC in the 1990s.[93]

The Trilateral Commission, which was founded in 1973, saw the current geopolitical situation in an entirely different light. One of its founders, Zbigniew Brzezinski, became Carter's National Security adviser. During the 2008 campaign, he was a senior foreign policy adviser to Obama. As the director of the Commission from 1973 to 1976, he contributed to developing its perspective on foreign affairs. In the Commission's view, the American Century was definitively over. US absolute supremacy had been superseded by 'complex interdependency' that necessitated a transformation of American foreign policy, which should focus on human rights and the helping of developing countries to achieve economic growth. The Trilateral Commission was determined to shift the focus of US foreign policy from the East–West axis of the Cold War and confront pressing North–South issues such as resource scarcity and the environment.[94]

Carter had no foreign policy experience of consequence when he became president. However, during the early days of his candidacy, he sought out the Trilateral Commission for advice on foreign policy.

Although he never said as much, Carter's 1977 speech on human rights and the 1979 malaise speech were an attempt to move beyond the tired nostrums of American exceptionalism and learn to live with limits and accept the end of US supremacy. This was, arguably, part of the lesson of Vietnam.

The initial reaction to the malaise speech was positive. However, in the long term, the speech came to be seen by many as defeatist. In an amazing about face, Carter essentially renounced his own speech six months later. In his State of the Union Address on 23 January 1980, in response to the Soviet invasion of Afghanistan, he made access to Middle East oil a cornerstone of his foreign policy:

> Let our position be absolutely clear: an attempt by any outside force to gain control of the Persian Gulf region will be regarded as an assault on the vital interests of the United States of America, and such an assault will be repelled by any means necessary, including military force.[95]

Carter authorized the establishment of the Central Command (CENTCOM), to control the oil flow from the Persian Gulf, shortly thereafter. The Carter Doctrine has since 1980 served as the justification for US intervention in the region.[96]

Ronald Reagan, who became the Republican nominee in 1980 and defeated Carter resoundingly in the general election, had nothing but contempt for a foreign policy that imposed limits on US power. Carter's attempt to move beyond the precepts of American exceptionalism was derailed on two fronts – by Soviet aggression in Afghanistan and by Reagan Republicans.

After the foreign policy disasters of the Bush years, Obama has the opportunity to continue the dismantling of the ideology of American exceptionalism that Carter began thirty years ago. His foreign policy rhetoric might at first glance not lend itself to a thorough reevaluation of the US role in the world. In his foreign policy speeches, Obama has consistently employed phrases conducive to the notion of an American exceptionalism. Nevertheless, I would argue, there are indications that Obama is moving – however surreptitiously – towards the formulation of a US foreign policy that, like Carter's initial policies, might portend a turning away from the idea of a Global War on Terror comparable to that of World War II or the Cold War, to a recognition of the limits of power in a post-American century.

As Andrew Bacevich has observed,

> when it comes to foreign policy, the fundamental divide
> in American politics today is not between left and right
> but between those who subscribe to the myth of the
> 'American Century' and those who do not.[97]

The question is to what extent Obama subscribes to this
myth. His foreign policy pronouncements would indicate
that he believes the US to be, as he put it, the 'last, best
hope on earth'. However, there are also signs that Obama
is willing to adapt to the geopolitics of the twenty-first
century.

In his address to Congress and the nation on 24 February,
Obama used the term 'American Century' in looking to
the future. Rhetorically, it would have been tantamount
to political suicide if he had announced the end of the
American Century, much less American exceptionalism.
However, his blueprint for a new American Century dif-
fered markedly from that proposed by the PNAC more than
a decade ago:

> The only way this century will be another American
> Century is if we confront at last the price of our depend-
> ence on oil and the high cost of health care; the schools
> that aren't preparing our children and the mountain of
> debt they stand to inherit. That is our responsibility.[98]

There were clear echoes of not only FDR and LBJ but also
of Jimmy Carter, in Obama's words. Like Carter, Obama
addressed a nation whose confidence was shaken. Short-
term profligacy had replaced long-term prosperity. He
spoke at length of the need for a complete overhaul of
US energy policy, much as Carter had done thirty years
before. In his address, Obama set forth proposals for the
expansion of renewable energy in the building of a new

energy economy. His energy-related appointments signal a break with the Bush administration's relative neglect of the issues of dependence on foreign oil as well as the threat of global warming. Obama's choice for Secretary of Energy, Steven Chu, a Nobel Laureate in physics, has long been an advocate of alternative sources of energy to reduce US dependence on the import of foreign oil. Obama also appointed Todd Stern, who worked with John Podesta at the liberal Center for American Progress, as his special envoy on climate change. Stern had served as the Clinton administration's top negotiator at the Kyoto talks on global warming and will lead the US delegation at the UN Climate Conference in Copenhagen in December 2009.

Conservative *New York Times* columnist David Brooks remembered interviewing an exhausted Obama on the campaign trail in 2007. In an attempt to keep the conversation going, Brooks asked Obama if he had ever read the work of Reinhold Niebuhr. According to Brooks, Obama immediately brightened and replied that Niebuhr was one of his favorite philosophers. When pressed to say what he had learned from Niebuhr, Obama said:

I take away the compelling idea that there's serious evil in the world, and hardship and pain. And we should be humble and modest in our belief we can eliminate those things. But we shouldn't use that as an excuse for cynicism and inaction. I take away . . . the sense we have to make these efforts knowing they are hard, and not swinging from naïve idealism to bitter realism.[99]

In *The Irony of American History*, Niebuhr warned of the inherent danger in 'our dreams of managing history'.[100] Obama clearly agrees with this sentiment. His notion of bending the arc of history assumes human agency as well as significant constraints. It is, on the other hand, diametrically opposed to the nameless Bush senior official interviewed by Ron Suskind, who saw Bush and his foreign policy staff as 'history's actors'. Bush himself lent credence to this view in his second inaugural speech, conceiving of history as having 'a visible direction, set by liberty and the Author of Liberty'.[101]

Carter's post-presidential humanitarian work provides another example for a post-exceptionalist Obama foreign policy. The Carter Center has been fighting a war against poverty and disease in Africa for some time. Through its efforts, the insidious disease of river blindness caused by worms has almost been eliminated. This is another kind of war from Bush's global War on Terror. As *New York Times* columnist Nicholas Kristof notes, Carter's war not only improves the lives of the poor and sick, it rehabilitates the US image in the world. While working in Ethiopia, Carter told Kristof that he would prefer war on malaria to war with Iran.[102]

A vision for a new US foreign policy for the twenty-first century might resemble the kind of liberal internationalism proposed by Roosevelt and Churchill in the Atlantic Charter in 1941 and consolidated at the end of the war with the Bretton Woods agreement, the establishment of the United Nations and NATO, and the Nuremberg trials – without, however, the pervasive American exceptionalist idea that the US necessarily has to take on a leadership role. The emphasis would be more on cooperation and interchange of ideas. A liberal internationalism for the twenty-first century would be based on the judicious use of 'smart power', as Hillary Clinton declared in her confirmation hearings, a willingness to forge alliances on national security issues, dignity promotion, climate change and a focus on deep cultural knowledge and development assistance such as microfinancing. As a rooted cosmopolitan who has seen the US from the outside, Obama has the potential to renew US foreign policy for the Post-American Century.

What Elizabeth Borgwardt calls the Zeitgeist of 1945,

which she defines as a 'new spirit' that 'produced a brief vogue for all things multilateral and cosmopolitan', may well animate US foreign policy in the twenty-first century.[103] The spirit of multilateralism that prevailed in the immediate postwar period was, according to the journalist E. B. White, directly linked to 'the successful model of America's polyglot, overpopulated cities'.[104] Chicago, the site of the Columbian World Exposition which promoted the idea of the inevitable progress of Western civilization, has been transformed into just such a polyglot metropolis, and is where the itinerant Obama became rooted.

A cosmopolitan American national identity actively promoted by a rooted cosmopolitan president will inevitably have an impact on notions of American exceptionalism that elide national differences in favour of an us-versus-them worldview. As Thomas Bender has argued, presenting 'a cosmopolitan appreciation of American participation in a history larger than itself' encourages humility and affirms transnational social solidarities.[105]

Furthermore, cosmopolitanism can function as a bulwark against the cultural myopia that has plagued American foreign policy since 1898, by nurturing deep knowledge of other societies. Instead of seeing cosmopolitanism as a threat of disunion, Americans could regard it as an opportunity to become citizens of the world even as they maintain their allegiance to the US.

Epilogue: 20 January 2009

Barack Obama became the forty-fourth president of the United States on Tuesday, 20 January 2009. The preceding three-day weekend was designed as a prelude to the inauguration. The four days, starting the previous Saturday and culminating with his inauguration on the 20th, ushered in the Obama era. These days were carefully choreographed to provide not only a sense of history, but a sense of how the arc of history could be bent to a better future.

On Saturday Obama boarded a train in Philadelphia that took him to his new home in Washington. Sunday was given over to a concert at the Lincoln Memorial. Monday was meant as a day devoted to public service. Each day was steeped in history, underscoring Obama's keen appreciation of the salience of the past in looking to the future.

Even though Dwight D. Eisenhower was the last president to take a train trip to Washington, Obama's journey to the nation's capital was an abridged version of the one that Abraham Lincoln embarked on from his home in Springfield, Illinois, on 11 February 1861, the day before his fifty-second birthday. It was in Springfield that Obama had launched his campaign for the presidency in February 2007, almost two years earlier. When Lincoln left for Washington, seven slave states had already left the union. Just one week earlier, these states had constituted the Confederate States of America, with Jefferson Davis as president.

The first leg of Lincoln's trip was replete with rallies and parades greeting the president-elect. However, advisers and military and civilian officials were concerned for his safety, not least because of rumours of an assassination plot in Baltimore. Lincoln was persuaded to make the rest of his journey from Harrisburg, Pennsylvania, via Philadelphia and Baltimore, under the cloak of secrecy and heightened security. He arrived in Washington on 23 February, weeks before the inauguration took place.

Obama chose to start his short, but highly visible journey in Philadelphia. It was there, only ten months earlier, that he had given his speech on race and had spoken of the Founding Fathers meeting in the nation's first capital to discuss the Constitution. Now, poised to assume the presidency, Obama went even further back in history. It was in Philadelphia that the Declaration of Independence was approved by the Continental Congress. The 'perserverance and idealism' displayed by the founders in 1776 should serve as inspiration to overcome the challenges that lay ahead. Obama called for a 'a new declaration of independence, not just in our nation, but in our own lives – from ideology and small thinking, prejudice and bigotry – an appeal not to our easy instincts but to our better angels.'[1]

Along the 137-mile route, the man born in the last state to enter the union stopped in Delaware, the first state to ratify the Constitution, to pick up Vice President-elect Joseph Biden. Stopping in Baltimore, Obama recalled another event in American history that tested the resolve of the new nation, the defence of Baltimore at Fort McHenry against the British in 1814 – an event that produced the national anthem. Arriving at Union Station in Washington in the early evening, Obama went directly to his motorcade.

Several times during the trip, Obama repeated a phrase from the very end of Lincoln's first inaugural address, appealing to 'the better angels' of Americans to forego 'prejudice and bigotry' and overcome the problems that lay ahead. In his constant effort to evoke Lincoln as a guiding light to future endeavours, Obama wilfully ignored the fact that Lincoln's first inaugural hardly constituted the kind of progress he was referring to. Indeed, Lincoln's first inaugural was concerned with saving the union, not abolishing slavery. Given the tenor of Lincoln's remarks, it was perhaps fitting that the man who administered the oath of office was none other than Chief Justice Roger Taney, who had presided over the Dred Scott case in 1857. In that rather infamous decision, Taney had offered an interpretation of the Declaration of Independence that excluded African Americans from the phrase 'all men are created equal'. As Taney put it, 'the enslaved African race were not intended to be included, and formed no part of the people who framed and adopted this declaration.' Taney concluded that African Americans, free or unfree, were not entitled to be citizens of the US and 'had no rights which the white man was bound to respect'.

Despite this setback, the abolitionist Frederick Douglass was optimistic about the future, thinking that the decision would bring the issue of slavery to the attention of the nation and therefore speed its demise. His disappointment at Lincoln's inaugural was therefore all the more intense. Lincoln began by reassuring the slave South that he had no intention whatsover of abolishing slavery. Furthermore, he made it clear that he had no quarrel with the Constitutional provision of the Fugitive Slave law, which had been strengthened by the Fugitive Slave Act of 1850. Lincoln expressed his support for a Thirteenth Amendment that was the diametrical opposite of the one ratified after the Civil War. His foremost concern was the fate of the union and his aim was to preserve it at all costs, even if it also meant preserving slavery. The sentiments expressed in appealing to the 'better angels' and the 'bonds of affection' (that Obama had quoted in his victory speech in November) were conciliatory gestures designed to appease the slave South, and to urge the states that had seceded to return to the union. Douglass contemplated emigrating to the second republic in the Americas, Haiti, after reading the speech.[2]

It is ironic that Obama, in his effort to get beyond partisan politics, would choose to draw on Lincoln's first inaugural address, which spoke of reconciliation between North and South by accepting the continuation of slavery. Obama's remarks on his journey from Philadelphia struck the same tones of the steady march of progress over injustice that he had used so effectively during the campaign. Lincoln's first inaugural address demonstrated that even the president who became revered as the man who freed the slaves was prepared, at the start of his presidency, to defend a setback for the abolitionist cause.

On the same day Obama took an old-fashioned train ride into the nation's capital, he released a video on YouTube announcing the conversion of his campaign organization, Obama for America, into Organizing for America. The brief message was an appeal to those who had worked to elect him to continue to help bring about the changes Obama had talked about during the campaign. He ended on a cryptic note, saying merely that information about the new organization would be forthcoming. His call for national service echoed President Kennedy's most-quoted line from his inaugural address, 'Ask not what your country can do for you, ask what you can do for your country'. Obama planned to use his email list of 13 million names to forge an organization working within the Democratic National Committee under its new head, Virginia governor Tim Kaine, to provide grass roots support for his political agenda. Obama dedicated the federal holiday marking Martin Luther King, Jr's birthday to promote national service. He visited wounded troops at the Walter Reed Medical Center, and then went to a shelter for homeless teenagers. Together with Martin Luther King III, Obama grabbed a paint roller to help renovate the shelter.

In a major speech in Denver in July 2008, Obama had outlined what he meant by national service. He linked his own biography with the larger American story, as he had done so effectively before, but this time emphasized how the call to national service was essential for an enlightened citizenry.

He told his audience to reject the false divide between the 'stories' of day-to-day life and the workings of the wider world. It is by 'stepping into the currents of history' that citizens can help shape the nation's future. He excoriated the Bush administration for passing up the opportunity to mobilize Americans in the wake of 9/11 – instead of a call to national service, they were told to shop. In that spirit, he pledged to expand AmeriCorps, an organization for local, state and national service, and the Peace Corps for foreign service. He also provided some initiatives of his own. He assured his audience that, if he became president, he would set up an Energy Corps 'to conduct renewable energy and environmental cleanup projects in their neighborhoods'. He closed with the thought that national service could contribute to 'the arc of history bending toward justice'.[3]

On the following day, the Lincoln Memorial provided the backdrop for a day of words and music billed as We Are One, a theme clearly inspired by Obama's speech at the Democratic National Convention less than five years earlier that propelled him to the national stage. The concert was a hodgepodge of musical styles and traditions, punctuated by short speeches and recitations by various actors and public figures.

The Lincoln Memorial was an appropriate venue for a concert celebrating not only the election of the first African American president but, with the theme We Are One, an end to the divisions that had characterized the eight years of Bush. A measure of the change that had taken place in the course of the twentieth century could be gauged by looking back at the ceremonies in 1922 that were held to mark the opening of the Memorial. African Americans and whites were seated separately for the event. The organizers had invited Robert Russa Moton, who had taken over the leadership of the Tuskegee Institute after the death of its founder Booker T. Washington in 1915, to give a speech at the opening. He was, however, required to submit a draft of the speech to the organizing committee. The committee decided to strike the following line that they found particularly incendiary:

My fellow citizens, in the great name which we honor here today, I say unto you that this memorial which we erect in token of our veneration is but a hollow mockery, a symbol of hypocrisy, unless we together can make real in our national life, in every state and in every section, the things for which he died.[4]

After a short invocation by the openly gay Episcopalian bishop from New Hampshire, V. Gene Robinson, a military band played Aaron Copland's *Fanfare for the Common Man*. The short piece, which Copland composed in 1943, has been referred to as an anthem for the New Deal.[5] Especially during the latter part of the presidential campaign, when the financial crisis became uppermost in the minds of voters, the idea of a new New Deal was often evoked. Playing the Copland piece only days before the inauguration of a president who was committed to the kind of public investment that brought back memories of the New Deal seemed a fitting prelude for things to come.

Queen Latifah conjured up memories of another New Deal legacy. She reminded the audience of an event that occurred on the steps of the Lincoln Memorial only seventy years before. In 1939, the Daughters of the American Revolution had refused to allow singer Marion Anderson to perform at an integrated concert at Constitution Hall. The first lady, Eleanor Roosevelt, arranged for Anderson to give an open-air concert at the Lincoln Memorial. As Queen Latifah spoke, giant screens set up along the Mall showed Anderson performing 'My Country 'Tis of Thee' at the Lincoln Memorial in 1939.

Another prominent theme was the struggle for racial justice. The actor Samuel L. Jackson told the story of Rosa

Parks, whose refusal to give up her seat to a white man on a bus in Montgomery, Alabama in 1955 sparked the Civil Rights movement. Predictably, the concert ended with all presenters and performers providing backup to Beyoncé's rendition of 'America the Beautiful'. However, it was the song preceding this one that best expressed the new mood. Standing in front of a choir, Bruce Springsteen introduced Pete Seeger who, along with Springsteen and Seeger's grandson Tao Rodriguez led the crowd in a rousing singalong of what Springsteen called 'the best song ever written about our nation' – Woody Guthrie's classic 'This Land Is Your Land'. At eighty-nine, Seeger was the oldest performer on stage that day. What made the performance especially poignant was that Seeger restored two verses to the song that were often omitted in more sanitized versions.

> As I was walkin' – I saw a sign there
> And that sign said – private property
> But on the other side . . . it didn't say nothin!
> Now that side was made for you and me!

> In the squares of the city – In the shadow of the steeple
> Near the relief office – I see my people
> And some are grumblin' and some are wonderin'
> If this land's still made for you and me.

More than any other song performed at the concert, Guthrie's Depression-era outcry against injustice, written in 1940 in response to Irving Berlin's 'God Bless America', was a poignant reminder of a time of hardship that once again had visited the US.

Even though Obama ostensibly struck a conciliatory tone in his inaugural address on 20 January, talking of putting past grievances aside, there was no mistaking his implicit rebuke of the policies of the man sitting directly behind him. After a brief thank-you to Bush for his service to the country,

Obama launched into a litany of the unfinished business that constituted the former president's disservice to his country. Towards the end of his presidency, Jimmy Carter had warned his countrymen of a 'crisis of confidence' afflicting the nation. Carter had the misfortune of governing in the wake of the ignominy of Watergate, the humiliation of Vietnam and the shock of the oil crisis. In his very first statement as president, Barack Obama echoed Carter in talking of the 'sapping of confidence' and the 'gathering clouds and raging storms' of crisis. Without ever referring to the Bush administration by name, the new president nevertheless made it clear that he intended to break with the failed policies of the past.

During his campaign, Obama was criticized for saying that 'Reagan changed the trajectory of America . . . He put us on a fundamentally different path because the country was ready for it.' In his inaugural address (which was criticized for having no memorable lines – or soundbites, in modern parlance), however, he took issue with the one line that many took away from Reagan's first inaugural, that government was the problem, not the solution. In his State of the Union Address in 1996, Clinton seemed to accept the premise of Reagan's argument by declaring that 'the era of big government is over'. Obama took a different course. It was not a question of big or small government but a government that works. An effective government was a far cry from Reagan's idea of the less government, the better. Obama went on to outline the responsibilities of government – 'whether it helps families find jobs at a decent wage, care they can afford, a retirement that is dignified.' The conservative belief in an unfettered market was also brought into question. 'Without a watchful eye,' Obama proclaimed, 'the market can spin out of control.'[6]

On foreign policy, Obama demonstrated that he had absorbed the teachings of Reinhold Niebuhr. Declaring his firm belief that 'our power grows through its prudent use',

Obama rejected the false choice 'between our safety and our ideals'. In yet another swipe at the previous administration, Obama reached out to the Muslim world by saying that he sought 'a new way forward, based on mutual interest and mutual respect.'[7]

The new president recognized that progress in history was achieved through the values that had always sustained Americans. These included not only hard work, honesty and fair play, but tolerance and curiosity as well. In looking to the future, Obama asked Americans 'to choose our better history'. At the end of the address, Obama looked to the beginning of the history of the American nation to help them do so. He chose not the era of Lincoln and the Civil War, which many no doubt expected, given the theme of the inaugural, 'A New Birth of Freedom'. Obama reached further back into the past, to the birth of the American nation in 1776. No doubt Obama had read or at least heard of popular historian David McCullough's book *1776*, which recounts that fateful year, calling it the darkest in all of American history.[8] It was towards the end of that year that the Continental Army, depleted by desertions and demoralized by succesive defeats, gathered across the Delaware River from New Jersey. In order to boost morale among the weary troops, their commander, George Washington, had an essay by Thomas Paine read to them. Without mentioning Paine by name, Obama read an excerpt from *The American Crisis*:

> Let it be told to the future world . . . that in the depth of winter, when nothing but hope and virtue could survive . . . that the city and the country, alarmed at one common danger, came forth to meet [it].[9]

In the months leading up to his election, Lincoln and Roosevelt were often referred to as presidents who led the US in times of war and economic crisis. Obama was taking office faced with two wars and an overstretched military, and an economic crisis, the likes of which had not been seen since the Great Depression. By evoking the dark days of December 1776, Obama conveyed the gravity of the current situation. He ended by appealing to the endurance and perseverance of Americans to overcome this present time of crisis.

In his inaugural address, Obama spoke eloquently of the strength of 'our patchwork heritage' comprised of people of many religions as well as non-believers. One of the most striking visuals of the inauguration was of Obama's family sitting behind him listening intensely to his words. The day after the inauguration, the *New York Times* ran a portrait of the new first family.

> The family that produced Barack and Michelle Obama is black and white and Asian, Christian, Muslim and Jewish. They speak English; Indonesian; French; Cantonese; German; Hebrew; African languages including Swahili, Luo and Igbo; and even a few phrases of Gullah, the Creole dialect of the South Carolina Lowcountry. Very few are wealthy, and some – like Sarah Obama, the stepgrand-mother who only recently got electricity and running water in her metal-roofed shack – are quite poor.[10]

As Obama's half-sister Maya Soetero-Ng pointed out, the multicultural composition of the Obama extended family may have seemed unusual for the White House, but not in relation to the US.[11] It was as if the first family and the nation they represented were finally in sync.

In his annual message to Congress in 1862, one month before signing the Emancipation Proclamation, Abraham Lincoln wrote:

> Fellow-citizens, we cannot escape history. We, of this Congress and this administration, will be remembered

in spite of ourselves. No personal significance, or insignificance, can spare one or another of us. The fiery trial through which we pass, will light us down, in honor or dishonor, to the latest generation.[12]

As Lincoln well knew, the freedom to make history is limited by any number of constraints. Yet, as Barack Obama, inspired by the words of Martin Luther King, Jr, has so often said, the arc of history may point in one direction, but it is possible to bend it, if only slightly. It is this act of bending that produces lasting change.

As President Obama flew to Chicago for his first visit home after three weeks in office, he mused to reporters on Air Force One about his own chance to bend history:

> Leadership at those moments can help determine which direction that wave of change goes. I think it's very hard . . . for any single individual or politician to unleash historical momentum on its own. But I think when that historical wave is there, I think you can help guide it.[13]

Notes

Note: The astute reader will no doubt have noticed that some of the sources I used are followed by the word 'ebook'. During the writing of this book, I purchased a Kindle, Amazon.com's electronic reader. While enabling me to gain access to new books as they were published, the Kindle has one huge disadvantage for the academic scholar. The pages that appear on the screen are not numbered as in the print version, but rather are 'locations' with numbers entirely unrelated to any rational page sequence. I have therefore simply indicated where I have used an ebook in the text. I sincerely hope this does not prove too frustrating for the reader.

Introduction

1 Theodore Draper, *Present History* (New York: Vintage, 1984).
2 Richard Rorty, *Achieving Our Country: Leftist Thought in Twentieth-Century America* (Cambridge, MA: Harvard University Press, 1999), p. 106.

Prologue

1 J. Hector St. John de Crèvecoeur, *Letters from an American Farmer* (1782), etext: http://www.gutenberg.org/etext/4666.
2 This and all other references to Obama's speech are from Barack Obama, '2004 Democratic National Convention Keynote Address', at American Rhetoric: http://www.americanrhetoric.com/speeches/convention2004/barackobama2004dnc.htm.
3 David Brooks, Mark Shields and Richard Norton Smith, commentary on PBS, 'Critique Immediately Following Obama's '04 Convention Speech', at: http://technorati.com/videos/youtube.com%2Fwatch%3Fv%3DQEzrJ-k9vH0.
4 Juan Williams, *Enough: The Phony Leaders, Dead-End Movements, and Culture of Failure That Are Undermining Black America – and What We Can Do About It* (New York: Three Rivers Press, 2006). For an alternative view, see Michael Eric Dyson, *Is Bill Cosby Right? Or Has the Black Middle Class Lost its Mind?* (New York: Basic Civitas, 2005). Bill

Obama's America

Cosby, 'Address at the NAACP on the 50th Anniversary of Brown v. Board of Education' (17 May 2004) at American Rhetoric: http://www.americanrhetoric.com/speeches/billcosbypoundcakespeech.htm.

5 Barack Obama, *The Audacity of Hope: Thoughts on Reclaiming the American Dream* (New York: Crown, 2006), pp. 361–2.

6 Barack Obama, 'Remarks of Illinois State Sen. Barack Obama Against Going to War with Iraq' (2 October 2002): http://www.barackobama.com/pdf/warspeech.pdf.

Part One

1 Sociologist Todd Gitlin's description of presidential elections as 'quadrennial plebescites on who we are' is quoted in Eleanor Clift, 'Palin Reignites the Culture War' *Newsweek* (3 October 2008): http://www.newsweek.com/id/162151.

2 Michael Lind, *Made in Texas: George W. Bush and the Southern Takeover of American Politics* (New York: New America Books, 2003), p. 80.

3 Rick Perlstein, *Nixonland: The Rise of a President and the Fracturing of America* (New York: Scribner, 2008), p. 748.

4 David Brooks, 'Where's the Landslide?', *New York Times* (5 August 2008):http://www.nytimes.com/2008/08/05/opinion/05brooks.html.

5 Barack Obama, *Dreams from My Father: A Story of Race and Inheritance* (New York: Three Rivers Press, 2004), p. vii.

6 Amartya Sen, *Identity and Violence: The Illusion of Destiny* (New York: Norton, 2006).

7 The *New Yorker* cover, 'The Politics of Fear', can be accessed at: http://www.newyorker.com/online/covers/slideshow_blittcovers.

8 See 'Fight the Smears', at: http://www.fightthesmears.com/.

9 The photograph depicted Obama in the traditional dress of a Somali elder. In February 2008, the Obama campaign accused the Clinton campaign of circulating the photo. See Michael Powell, 'Photo of Obama in African Garb Emerges as Clinton Renews Attacks', *International Herald Tribune* (25 February 2008): http://www.iht.com/articles/2008/02/25/america/25webcamp.php.

10 Bob Herbert, 'Confronting the Kitchen Sink', *New York Times* (8 March 2008): http://www.nytimes.com/2008/03/08/opinion/08herbert.html. See also Eric Boehlert, 'Hillary Clinton, *60 Minutes* and the Muslim Question', *Media Matters* (11 March 2008): http://mediamatters.org/columns/200803110002.

Notes

11 Michael Dimock, 'Belief That Obama Is Muslim Durable, Bipartisan, But Most Likely to Sway Democrats' Pew Research Center (15 July 2008): http://pewresearch.org / pubs / 898 / belief-that-obama-is-muslim-is-bipartisan-but-most-likely-to-sway-democrats.

12 Jonathan Martin and Amie Parnes, 'McCain: Obama Not an Arab, Crowd Boos', *Politico* (10 October 2008): http://www.politico.com/news/stories/1008/14479.html.

13 Transcript of Colin Powell on *Meet the Press* (19 October 2008): http://www.msnbc.msn.com/id/27266223/page/2/.

14 Tim Jones, 'Barack Obama: Mother Not Just a Girl From Kansas' *Chicago Tribune* (27 March 2007): http://www.chicagotribune.com/news / politics / obama / chi-0703270151mar27-archive,0,2623808. story? page=1.

15 Obama, *The Audacity of Hope*, p. 204.

16 Ibid., pp. 203–4. See also Beliefnet on Obama's Faith: http://www.beliefnet.com/News/Politics/2008/03/Obamas-Faith-Rumor-Vs-Reality.aspx#1.

17 Beliefnet: 'John McCain: Constitution Established a "Christian Nation"': http://www.beliefnet.com / News / Politics / 2007 / 06/ John-Mccain-Constitution-Established-A-Christian-Nation.aspx.

18 The Pew Forum on Religion and Public Life, 'How the Faithful Voted': http://pewforum.org/docs/?DocID=367.

19 Diana Eck, *A New Religious America: How a 'Christian Country' has become the World's Most Religiously Diverse Nation* (New York: Harper, 2001), p. 4.

20 The Pew Forum on Religion and Public Life, *U.S. Religious Landscape Survey* (February 2008), p. 5.

21 Pew Forum, 'How the Faithful Voted'.

22 'Cokie Roberts on Obama's Vacation', *Media Matters* (10 August 2008): http://mediamatters.org/items/200808100001.

23 See the essays on Alaska and Hawaii in Matt Weiland and Sean Wilsey, *State By State: A Panoramic Portrait of America* (New York: Ecco, 2008).

24 See Stephen Kinzer, *Overthrow: America's Century of Regime Change From Hawaii to Iraq* (New York: Times Books, 2006), pp. 9–31.

25 'Remarks as Prepared for Delivery by Alaska Governor Sarah Palin – Republican National Convention' (3 September 2008): http://portal.gopconvention2008.com/speech/details.aspx?id=38.

26 Sahil Mahtani quoted in Marty Peretz, 'Palin and Pegler', *The New Republic* (13 September 2008): http://blogs.tnr.com/tnr/blogs/the_spine/archive/2008/09/13/palin-and-pegler.aspx.

27 Palin quoted in Sam Stein, 'Palin Explains What Parts of the Country Not "Pro-America"', *Huffington Post* (17 October 2008): http://

www.huffingtonpost.com/2008/10/17/palin-clarifies-what-part_n_135641.html.

28 Sam Stein, 'Michele Bachmann Channels McCarthy', *Huffington Post* (17 October 2008): http://www.huffingtonpost.com/2008/10/17/gop-rep-channels-mccarthy_n_135735.html.

29 Jennifer Bradley and Bruce Katz, 'Village Idiocy', *The New Republic* (8 October 2008): http://www.tnr.com/politics/story.html?id=504eadb7-fe17-4ca7-9b22-382b43990f34.

30 Kevin Pollard and Mark Mather, '10% of US Counties Now "Majority-Minority"', Population Reference Bureau: http://www.prb.org/Articles/2008/majority-minority.aspx.

31 Political Radar blog (7 November 2007): http://blogs.abcnews.com/politicalradar/2007/11/obama-says-flag.html.

32 Obama quoted in Jay Newton-Small, 'Obama's Flag Pin Flip-Flop?', *Time* (14 May 2008).

33 John Milton Cooper, 'The Election of 2000 at the Bar of History', in Jack N. Rakove, ed., *The Unfinished Election of 2000: Leading Scholars Examine America's Strangest Election* (New York: Basic Books, 2001), pp. 30–1.

34 A video and transcript of this ad is available at The Museum of the Moving Image, The Living Room Candidate: http://www.living-roomcandidate.org/commercials/2008.

35 Barack Obama, 'The America We Love' (30 June 2008): http://www.barackobama.com/2008/06/30/remarks_of_senator_barack_obam_83.php.

36 Ibid.

37 Barack Obama, 'A World That Stands as One', transcript: http://www.nytimes.com/2008/07/24/us/politics/24text-obama.html.

38 George F. Will, 'The Cosmopolitan', *Washington Post* (3 August 2008): http://www.washingtonpost.com/wp-dyn/content/article/2008/08/01/AR2008080102871.html.

39 Obama, 'A World That Stands as One'.

40 Kwame Anthony Appiah, *Cosmopolitanism: Ethics in a World of Strangers* (New York: Norton, 2006), pp. xvi–xvii.

41 Jonathan Hansen, *The Lost Promise of Patriotism: Debating American Identity 1890–1920* (Chicago: University of Chicago Press, 2003).

42 For a transcript of the exchange between Obama and Wurzelbacher, see Jake Tapper, ABC News, 'Political Punch' (14 October 2008): http://blogs.abcnews.com/politicalpunch/2008/10/spread-the-weal.html.

43 CNN: *The Situation Room* (31 October 2008): http://transcripts.cnn.com/TRANSCRIPTS/0810/31/sitroom.03.html.

Notes

44 Centre for Economic Performance, London School of Economics, 'Intergenerational Mobility in Europe and America' (April 2005): http://cep.lse.ac.uk/about/news/IntergenerationalMobility.pdf.

45 'Giuliani attacks democratic health care plans as "socialist"': http://edition.cnn.com/2007/POLITICS/07/31/giuliani.democrats/index.html.

46 R. Laurence Moore, *European Socialists and the American Promised Land* (New York: Oxford, 1970), pp. 17–18.

47 Quoted ibid., p. 115.

48 Steve Fraser and Gary Gerstle, *The Rise and Fall of the New Deal Order 1930–1980* (Princeton: Princeton University Press, 1989), p. ix.

49 Amity Shlaes, *The Forgotten Man: A New History of the Great Depression* (New York: HarperCollins, 2007), p. 7.

50 Patrick Buchanan, '1992 Republican National Convention Speech', The Internet Brigade: http://www.buchanan.org/pa-92-0817-mc.html.

51 Kristol quoted in Gary B. Nash et al., *History on Trial: Culture Wars and the Teaching of the Past* New York: Knopf, 1997), p. 7.

52 Samuel Huntington, *Who Are We? The Challenges to America's National Identity* (New York: Simon and Schuster, 2004), pp. 137, 19.

53 John Higham, *Strangers in the Land: Patterns of American Nativism 1860–1925* (New York: Atheneum, 1985), pp. 316–24.

54 See Noel Ignatiev, *How the Irish Became White* (London: Routledge, 1996).

55 W. E. B. Du Bois, *The Souls of Black Folk* (1903): http://www.bartleby.com/114/100.html.

56 See Ann Douglas, *Terrible Honesty: Mongrel Manhattan in the 1920s* (New York: Farrar, Straus and Giroux, 1995).

57 Steve Inskeep and Michele Norris, 'York Voters Express Post-Election Hopes, Fears', National Public Radio, *All Things Considered* (24 October 2008): http://www.npr.org/templates/story/story.php?storyId=96187966.

58 Lind, *Made in Texas*, p. 26.

59 Peter Applebome, *Dixie Rising*. See also Kevin Phillips, *American Theocracy* (New York: Viking, 2006), pp. 132–82.

60 Alex Johnson, 'Tennessee Ad Ignites Internal GOP Squabbling', *MSNBC* (25 October 2006): http://www.msnbc.msn.com/id/15403071.

61 Bob Herbert, 'Running While Black', *New York Times* (2 August 2008): http://www.nytimes.com/2008/08/02/opinion/02herbert.html?ref=opinion.

62 Obama, *The Audacity of Hope*, p. 233.

63 Ibid., p. 230.

64 Cosby, 'Address at the NAACP on the 50th Anniversary of Brown v. Board of Education'.
65 For two sides of the debate on black responsibility, see Dyson, *Is Bill Cosby Right?* And Williams, *Enough.*
66 Barack Obama, 'A More Perfect Union' (18 March 2008): http://my.barackobama.com/page/content/hisownwords.
67 Matt Bai, 'Is Obama the End of Black Politics?', *New York Times Magazine* (10 August 2008): http://www.nytimes.com/2008/08/10/magazine/10politics-t.html?em).
68 Barack Obama, 'Remarks at Selma Voting Rights Commemoration' (4 March 2007): http://www.barackobama.com/2007/03/04/selma_ voting_rights_march_comm.php.
69 Pew Research Center, 'Blacks See Growing Values Gap Between Poor and Middle Class' (13 November 2007): http://pewsocial-trends.org/pubs/700/black-public-opinion.
70 Barack Obama, 'Victory Speech' (4 November 2008), *Huffington Post*: http://www.huffingtonpost.com/2008/11/04/obama-victory-speech_n_141194.html.
71 Obama, *The Audacity of Hope*, p. 231.
72 Wood quoted in Gary Gerstle, *American Crucible: Race and Nation in the Twentieth Century* (Princeton: Princeton University Press), p. 349.
73 Mark Penn, *Microtrends: The Small Forces Behind Today's Big Changes* (London: Allen Lane, 2007), p. xv.
74 Joshua Green, 'The Front-Runner's Fall', *Atlantic Monthly* (September 2008): http://www.theatlantic.com / doc / 200809 / hillary-clinton-campaign/2.
75 A transcript of Obama's remarks can be found at Mark Halperin, 'The Page', *Time* (23 February 2008): http://thepage.time.com/transcript-of-obamas-remarks-at-san-francisco-fundraiser-sunday/.
76 Eli Saslow and Robert Barnes, 'In a More Diverse America, A Mostly White Convention', *Washington Post* (4 September 2008): http://www.washingtonpost.com/wp-dyn/content/article/2008/09/03/AR2008090303962.html.
77 John Judis, 'America the Liberal', *The New Republic* (5 November 2008).
78 Tom Tancredo, *In Mortal Danger: The Battle for America's Border and Security* (Nashville, TN: WND Books, 2006), p. 188.
79 Huntington, *Who Are We?*, p. 205.
80 Anthony Kwame Appiah, *Cosmopolitanism.*
81 Sen, *Identity and Violence.*
82 Tamar Jacoby, 'What it Means to be an American in the 21st Century', in Tamar Jacoby, ed., *Reinventing the Melting Pot: The New*

Notes

Immigrants and What It Means to be American (New York: Basic Books, 2004), p. 313.

83 See Perlstein, *Nixonland*, p. 46.
84 'Illinois Sen. Barack Obama's Announcement Speech', *Washington Post* (10 February 2007).
85 Barack Obama, 'Victory Speech in Grant Park' (4 November 2008): http://elections.nytimes.com/2008/results/president/speeches/obama-victory-speech.html.
86 Obama, *Dreams from My Father*, p. 133.
87 Ibid., 133.
88 See Janny Scott, 'Obama's Account of New York Years Differs from What Others Say', *New York Times* (20 October 2007).
89 Obama, *Dreams from My Father*, pp. 134–5.
90 Jason Fink, 'Obama's Years in New York Left Lasting Impression on Colleagues' (9 November 2008): http://weblogs.amny.com/entertainment/urbanite/blog/2008/11/obamas_years_in_new_york_left.html#more.
91 Obama, *Dreams from My Father*, pp. 139–40.
92 According to Ryan Lizza, Kaufman is an amalgam of Gerald Kellman and Mike Kruglik. See Lizza, 'The Agitator', *The New Republic* (19 March 2007).
93 Two studies focusing on the Great Migration are Nicolas Lemann, *The Promised Land: The Great Migration and How It Changed America* (New York: Knopf, 1991) and James Grossman, *Land of Hope: Chicago, Black Southerners and the Great Migration* (Chicago: University of Chicago Press, 1989).
94 Claude McKay, 'If We Must Die', *Harlem Shadows: The Poems of Claude McKay* (New York: Harcourt, Brace & Co., 1922).
95 Michael Eric Dyson, *I May Not Get There With You: The True Martin Luther King, Jr.* (New York: Free Press, 2000), pp. 80–3).
96 William Julius Wilson, *When Work Disappears: The World of the New Urban Poor* (New York: Knopf, 1996), p. 49).
97 On the Back of the Yards, see the entry in *Encyclopedia of Chicago History*: http://www.encyclopedia.chicagohistory.org/pages/99.html.
98 Barack Obama, 'Why Organize? Problems and Promise in the Inner City', in Peg Knoepfle, *After Alinsky: Community Organizing in Illinois* (Springfield: Institute for Public Affairs, 1990), pp. 35–40. Obama's article can be accessed at: http://www.edwoj.com/Alinsky/AlinskyObamaChapter1990.htm.
99 Ibid.
100 Saul Alinsky, *Rules for Radicals* (New York: Vintage, 1972), p. 26.
101 Ibid., p. 84.

102 Obama, 'Why Organize?'.
103 Wilson, *When Work Disappears*, p. xiii.
104 Ibid., pp. 48, 49.
105 LeAlan Jones and Lloyd Newman, *Our America: Life and Death on the South Side of Chicago* (New York: Scribner, 1997), p. 199.
106 Ibid., p. 163.
107 Obama, *Dreams from My Father*, p. 242. Obama has been accused of taking too much credit for his role in the fight to remove asbestos from Altgeld Gardens. One resident in particular, Hazel Johnson, has contested his version of events. See Letta Tayler and Keith Herbert, 'Obama forged path as Chicago community organizer', *Newsday* (2 March 2008).
108 Obama, *Dreams from My Father*, p. 170.
109 Michael Kranish, 'A Defining Time of Advocacy', *Boston Globe* (22 January 2008).
110 Moyers quoted in Nick Kotz, *Judgment Days: Lyndon Baines Johnson, Martin Luther King, Jr. and the Laws That Changed America* (New York: Houghton Mifflin, 2005), p. 154.
111 Adam Doster, 'Growing the Pie', *Illinois Times* (7 August 2008).
112 Obama, *The Audacity of Hope*, p. 36.
113 Leonard Steinhorn, *The Greater Generation: In Defense of the Baby Boom Legacy* (New York: St. Martin's Press, 2006).
114 Michael D. Hais and Morley Winograd, *Millennial Makeover: MySpace, YouTube, and the Future of American Politics* (New Brunswick: Rutgers University Press, 2008): ebook.
115 Alec MacGillis, 'Obama Camp Relying Heavily on Ground Effort', *Washington Post* (12 October 2008).
116 Ari Berman, 'The Dean Legacy', *The Nation* (28 February 2008).
117 Brevy Cannon, 'Center for Politics Post-Election Conference Dissects Why Obama Won', *University of Virginia Today* (25 November 2008): http://www.virginia.edu/uvatoday/newsRelease.php?id=7110).
118 Nedra Pickler, 'Obama's Political Team Out-Organized Clinton', *Associated Press* (24 May 2008).
119 Zack Exley, 'Obama Field Organizers Plot a Miracle', *Huffington Post* (27 August 2007).
120 Ibid.
121 Thurston Clarke, *The Last Campaign: Robert F. Kennedy and 82 Days that Inspired America* (New York: Henry Holt & Co., 2008): ebook.
122 Alec MacGillis, 'Obama Camp Relying Heavily on Ground Effort', *Washington Post* (12 October 2008).

Notes

123 See acorn.org.

124 Justin Rood, 'McCain ACORN Fears Overblown', *ABC News: The Blotter from Brian Ross* (16 October 2008): http://abcnews.go.com/Blotter/story?id=6049529.

125 See the Obama website 'Fight the Smears': http://www.fightthesmears.com/articles/20/acornrumor.

126 Markos Moulitsas Zuniga, *Taking On the System: Rules for Radical Change in a Digital Era* (New York: New American Library, 2008): ebook.

127 Matt Bai, *The Argument: Billionaires, Bloggers, and the Battle to Remake Democratic Politics* (New York: Penguin, 2007), pp. 126, 133, 138.

128 Sarah Lai Stirland, 'Inside Obama's Surging Net-Roots Campaign', *Wired* (3 March 2008): http://www.wired.com/politics/law/news/2008/03/obama_tools.

129 G. Calvin Mackenzie and Robert Weisbrot, *The Liberal Hour: Washington and the Politics of Change in the 1960s* (New York: Penguin, 2008), pp. 14–15.

130 Robert E. Scott, Carlos Salas, and Bruce Campbell, 'Revisiting NAFTA: Still Not Working for North America's Workers', *Economic Policy Institute* (28 September 2006): http://epi.3cdn.net/6def605657a958c3da_85m6ibu0h.pdf, pp. 2, 3.

131 Barack Obama, 'Keeping America's Promise' (13 February 2008): http://www.barackobama.com/2008/02/13/remarks_of_senator_barack_obam_50.php.

132 James Parks, 'Union Membership on the Rise', *AFL-CIO Now Blog* (25 January 2008).

133 Jeffrey M. Jones, 'Americans Remain Broadly Supportive of Labor Unions', *Gallup* (1 December 2008): http://www.gallup.com/poll/112717/Americans-Remain-Broadly-Supportive-Labor-Unions.aspx.

134 Press release, 15 February, at: seiu.org.

135 Andy Stern, 'Labor's New New Deal', *The Nation* (24 March 2008). See also Andy Stern, *A Country That Works: Getting America Back on Track* (New York: Free Press, 2006).

136 'Barack Obama on the Employee Free Choice Act': http://www.youtube.com/watch?v=_4qF213IceI.

137 Greg Sargent, 'Labor Leaders Hail Obama's Pick For Labor Secretary', *Talking Points Memo* (18 December 2008): http://tpmelectioncentral.talkingpointsmemo.com/2008/12/andy_stern_on_obamas_labor_sec.php.

138 Amanda Terkel, 'McConnell: Employee Free Choice Act will "fundamentally harm America and Europeanize America"', *Think Progress* (23 January 2009).

139 Thomas Frank, 'It's Time to Give Voters the Liberalism They Want', *Wall Street Journal* (18 November 2008).

140 Harley Shaiken, 'Stronger Unions Mean a Strong Middle Class', *Los Angeles Times* (17 February 2007).

141 Governor Romney Addresses CPAC: http://www.mittromney.com/News/Press-Releases/CPAC_Address.

142 Ibid.

143 Nick Taylor, *American-Made: The Enduring Legacy of the WPA: When FDR put the Nation to Work* (New York: Bantam, 2008).

144 American Society of Civil Engineers, *Report Card for America's Infrastructure*, available at: http://www.asce.org/reportcard/2005/index.cfm.

145 'Conservatives Cherry-Pick 1930s Unemployment Figures in Continued Assault on New Deal' *Media Matters* (3 December 2008): http://mediamatters.org/items/200812030014.

146 Richard Hofstadter, *The Age of Reform* (New York: Knopf, 1955).

147 William Greider, 'A "New" New Deal', *The Nation* (3 October 2005).

148 John M. Barry, *Rising Tide: The Great Mississippi Flood of 1927 and How It Changed America* (New York: Touchstone, 1997).

149 Bobby Jindal, 'Transcript of Gov. Jindal's GOP Response to Obama Speech', *CNN* (24 February 2009): http://edition.cnn.com/2009/POLITICS/02/24/sotn.jindal.transcript/.

150 Kristol quoted in Paul Krugman, *The Conscience of a Liberal* (New York: Norton, 2007), p. 228.

151 Caren Bohan, 'Bush Vetoes Popular Bill on Kids' Health Care', *Reuters* (3 October 2007): http://www.reuters.com/article/latestCrisis/idUSN03192027.

152 Ramesh Ponnuru and Richard Lowry, 'The Grim Truth', *National Review* (19 November 2007).

153 Paul Krugman, 'The Grim Truth', *New York Times* (1 December 2007): http://krugman.blogs.nytimes.com/2007/12/01/the-grim-truth/.

154 Robert Pear, 'Veto Risk Seen in Compromise on Child Health', *New York Times* (17 September 2007).

155 Robert Pear, 'Obama Signs Children's Health Insurance Bill', *Washington Post* (5 February 2009).

156 'Obama Delivers Remarks at Signing of SCHIP Legislation', *CQ Transcripts Wires*, Wednesday, 4 February 2009; 5:29 pm.

157 Barack Obama, 'Keeping Promises', Weekly Address (28 February 2009) at: http://www.whitehouse.gov/blog/09/02/28/Keeping-Promises/.

Notes

158 Jim Rutenberg, 'Liberal Groups Are Flexing New Muscle in Lobby Wars', *New York Times* (1 March 2009).

159 Jonah Goldberg, 'Invasion of the America Snatchers': http://www. nationalreview.com/goldberg/goldberg200505190810.asp.

160 Jon Meacham and Evan Thomas, 'We're All Socialists Now', *Newsweek* (16 February 2009).

161 Jeremy P. Jacobs, 'McConnell: Stimulus Would Lead to "Europeanization"', *The Hill's Blog Briefing Room* (10 February 2009).

162 David Leonhardt, 'More Than One Way to Take Over a Bank', *New York Times* (25 February 2009).

163 'Barack Announces Organizing for America', at: http://my. barackobama.com/page/community/post/stateupdates/gGxFj8.

164 Paul Krugman, 'Bad Faith Economics', *New York Times* (26 January 2009).

165 Carol E. Lee, 'Team Obama Mobilizing E-Mail List', *Politico* (23 January 2009).

166 Barack Obama, 'Remarks by President Barack Obama at the House Democratic Caucus Issues Conference', *LexisNexis News* (5 February 2009).

167 David M. Herszenhorn, 'A Smaller, Faster Stimulus Plan, but Still With a Lot of Money', *New York Times* (14 February 2009).

168 Barack Obama, 'Remarks of President Barack Obama – Address to Joint Session of Congress' (24 February 2009): http://www.whitehouse.gov/the_press_office/Remarks-of-President-Barack-Obama-Address-to-Joint-Session-of-Congress/.

169 Emmanuel Saez, 'Striking It Richer: The Evolution of Top Incomes in the United States', Department of Economics, University of California (15 March 2008): http://emlab.berkeley.edu/~saez/saez-UStopincomes-2006prel.pdf.

170 Perlstein, *Nixonland*, p. 277.

171 Hubert Humphrey, '1948 Democratic Convention Address', at American Rhetoric: http://www.americanrhetoric.com/speeches/huberthumphey1948dnc.html.

172 Kevin Phillips, *The Emerging Republican Majority* (New Rochelle: Arlington House, 1969), p. 286.

173 Ibid., p. 461.

174 Ibid., Map 47, p. 472.

175 Ibid., p. 473.

176 John Judis and Ruy Texeira, *The Emerging Democratic Majority* (New York: Scribner, 2002).

177 John Judis, 'America the Liberal', *The New Republic* (5 November 2008).

178 John Judis and Ruy Texeira, 'Back to the Future', *The American Prospect* (19 June 1977).
179 Andrew Kohut, 'Post-Election Perspectives' *Pew Research Center for the People and the Press* (13 November 2008): http://pewresearch. org/pubs/1039/post-election-perspectives.
180 Stanley Greenberg and Robert Borosage, 'The Change Election Awaiting Change', The Campaign for America's Future: http:// www.ourfuture.org/report/2008114507/change-election-2008.
181 Teddy Davis and Ferdous Al-Faruque, 'McConnell: GOP Becoming "Regional Party"', *ABC News: The Note* (29 January 2009).
182 G. Calvin Mackenzie and Robert Weisbrot, op. cit., p. 3.

Part Two

1 James Traub, 'Is (His) Biography (Our) Destiny?', *New York Times Sunday Magazine* (4 November 2007).
2 Transcript of Obama's Interview with Al-Arabiya: htp://www. alarabiya.net/articles/2009/01/27/65096.html.
3 'Obama Touts Life in Asia, Kenyan Background', AFP (19 November 2007): http://afp.google.com / article / ALeqM5gRVlNCfrTmHF-OGaFGEQyKgQI2Pg.
4 Fareed Zakaria, 'The Power of Personality', *Newsweek* (24 December 2007).
5 Obama, *Dreams from My Father*, p.100.
6 Michael Hirsh, 'Worlds Apart', *Newsweek* (6 October 2008).
7 See Robert Dallek, *John F. Kennedy: An Unfinished Life* (London: Penguin, 2004), pp. 49–66.
8 Godfrey Hodgson, 'The Foreign Policy Establishment', in Steve Fraser and Gary Gerstle, eds, *Ruling America: A History of Power and Wealth in a Democracy* (Cambridge, MA: Harvard University Press, 2005), pp. 217, 222.
9 Frances FitzGerald, *Way Out There in the Blue: Reagan, Star Wars and the End of the Cold War* (New York: Simon and Schuster, 2000), pp. 75–9.
10 Lind, *Made in Texas*, pp. 145–59.
11 US Census Bureau, 'Hawaii: Race and Hispanic Origin: 1900 to 1990': http://www.census.gov/population/www/documentation/ twps0056/tab26.pdf.
12 Richard Wright, *The Color Curtain: A Report on the Bandung Conference* (Cleveland and New York: The World Publishing Company, 1956), pp. 12, 220.
13 Amanda Ripley, 'Barack Obama's Mother', *Time* (9 April 2008) and

Notes

Janny Scott, 'A Free-Sprited Wanderer Who Set Obama's Path', *New York Times* (14 March 2008).

14 'Hillary Clinton's Opening Remarks at Her Senate Confirmation Hearing', *Real Clear Politics* (13 January 2009): http://www.realclearpolitics.com/articles/2009/01/clintons_opening_remarks_at_he.html.

15 Hillary Clinton, 'Setting Forth a Clear Path for USAID To Regain a Global Leadership Role in Development Assistance' (23 January 2009): http://www.state.gov/secretary/rm/2009a/01/115325.htm).

16 Obama, *Dreams from My Father*, pp. 47, 50, 51.

17 Ibid., pp. 182–3.

18 Maverick Chen, 'Punahou's Connection With China', *China.org.cn* (18 November 2008): http://www.china.org.cn/international/cultural_sidelines/2008-11/18/content_16786568.htm.

19 Jennifer Steinhauer, 'Charisma and a Search for Self in Obama's Hawaii Childhood', *New York Times* (17 March 2007).

20 Barack Obama, 'An Honest Government, A Hopeful Future', speech delivered at the University of Nairobi, 28 August 2006: http://wrageblog.org/2009/01/19/president-elect-obamas-2006-speech-at-the-university-of-nairobi/. Caroline Elkins, *Imperial Reckoning: The Untold Story of Britain's Gulag in Kenya* (New York: Henry Holt, 2005): ebook.

21 Obama, 'An Honest Government, A Hopeful Future'.

22 Barack Obama, 'Selma Voting Rights March Commemoration' (4 March 2007): http://www.barackobama.com/2007/03/04/selma_voting_rights_march_comm.php; Elana Schor, 'The other Obama–Kennedy connection', *The Guardian* (10 January 2008) and Michael Dobbs, 'Obama–Kennedy Link Falls Short in Fact Check', *Washington Post* (30 March 2008).

23 Mary L. Dudziak, *Cold War Civil Rights* (Princeton: Princeton University Press, 2000), p. 230.

24 Larry Rohter, 'Obama Says Real-Life Experience Trumps Rivals' Foreign Policy Credits', *New York Times* (10 April 2008).

25 Frederick Jackson Turner, 'The Significance of the Frontier in American History', etext at: http://xroads.virginia.edu/~Hyper/TURNER/.

26 Robert Rydell, *All the World's a Fair: Visions of Empire at American International Expositions, 1876–1916* (Chicago: University of Chicago Press, 1984), pp. 38–72.

27 Douglass quoted in William McFeely, *Frederick Douglass* (New York: Norton, 1991), p. 371.

28 Stephen Kinzer, *Overthrow: America's Century of Regime Change From Hawaii to Iraq* (New York: Henry Holt, 2006), pp. 9–31.
29 Albert Beveridge, 'In Support of an American Empire': http://www.mtholyoke.edu/acad/intrel/ajb72.htm.
30 Ibid.
31 Beveridge quoted in opening 'Newsreel' of John Dos Passos's trilogy *USA* (New York: Modern Library, 1937), p. 4.
32 Brooks Adams, *America's Economic Supremacy* (New York: Macmillan, 1900) and William Appleman Williams, *The Tragedy of American Diplomacy* (1959; New York: Norton, 1988), p. 52.
33 William T. Stead, *The Americanization of the World, or The Trend of the Twentieth Century* (New York: Horace Markley, 1901).
34 Francis Fukuyama, 'The End of History?', *The National Interest* (Summer 1989).
35 Charles Krauthammer, 'The Unipolar Moment', *Foreign Affairs* (1990/91).
36 'Excerpts from 1992 draft "defense planning guidance"', PBS: http://www.pbs.org/wgbh/pages/frontline/shows/iraq/etc/wolf.html See also James Mann, *Rise of the Vulcans: The History of Bush's War Cabinet* (New York: Viking, 2004), pp. 208–15.
37 PNAC, Statement of Principles: http://www.newamericancentury.org/statementofprinciples.htm.
38 Ron Suskind, 'Faith, Certainty and the Presidency of George W. Bush', *New York Times Magazine* (17 October 2004).
39 Reinhold Niebuhr, *The Irony of American History* (1952; Chicago: University of Chicago Press, 2008), p. 143.
40 Paul Kennedy, *The Rise and Fall of the Great Powers* (New York: Random House, 1987).
41 Paul Kennedy, 'American Power is on the Wane', *Wall Street Journal* (14 January 2009).
42 Charles Kupchan, *The End of the American Era: U.S. Foreign Policy and the Geopolitics of the Twenty-First Century* (New York: Knopf, 2002), p. xvii.
43 Joseph E. Stiglitz and Linda J. Bilmes, *The Three Trillion Dollar War: The True Cost of the Iraq Conflict* (New York: Norton, 2008).
44 National Intelligence Council, *Mapping the Global Future* (Washington, DC: US Government Printing Office, 2004): http://www.foia.cia.gov/2020/2020.pdf. National Intelligence Council, *Global Trends 2025: A Transformed World* (Washington, DC: US Government Printing Office, 2008): www.dni.gov/nic/NIC_2025_project.html.
45 National Intelligence Council, *Global Trends 2025*, p. vi.
46 Ibid., p. 23.

47 Ibid., pp. iv, 28.
48 Richard N. Haass, 'The Age of Nonpolarity', *Foreign Affairs* (May/ June 2008).
49 Ibid.
50 Fareed Zakaria, *The Post-American World* (New York: Norton, 2008): ebook.
51 Pareg Khanna, *The Second World: How Emerging Powers are Redefining Global Competition in the Twenty-first Century* (New York: Random House, 2008) and Mark Leonard, *Why Europe will Run the 21st Century* (London: Fourth Estate, 2005).
52 Princeton Project on National Security, *Forging a World of Liberty Under Law* (The Woodrow Wilson School of Public and International Affairs, 2006), p. 17.
53 Ibid., p. 21.
54 Ibid., p. 26.
55 Greg Grandin, *Empire's Workshop: Latin America, the United States, and the Rise of the New Imperialism* (New York: Metropolitan Books, 2006), p. 4.
56 'Remarks by the President at Summit of the Americas Working Session' (21 April 2001): http://www.whitehouse.gov/news/releases/2001/04/20010423-9.html.
57 Barack Obama, 'A New Partnership for the Americas' (printed in house for Obama for America, 2008).
58 Niall Ferguson, 'Geopolitical Consequences of the Credit Crunch' (21 September 2008): http://www.niallferguson.com/site/FERG/Templates/ArticleItem.aspx?pageid=195.
59 Robert Kaplan, *Hog Pilots, Blue Water Grunts: The American Military in the Air, at Sea, and on the Ground* (New York: Random House, 2007), p. 48.
60 Suzanne Nossel, 'Smart Power', *Foreign Affairs* (March/April 2004).
61 Glenn Kessler, 'Clinton Criticized for Not Trying to Force China's Hand', *Washington Post* (21 February 2009); Mark Landler, 'Clinton Praises Indonesian Democracy', *New York Times* (18 February 2009).
62 Council on Foreign Relations, 'The Shanghai Cooperation Organization': http://www.cfr.org/publication/10883/#3.
63 'Remarks of Senator Barack Obama: AIPAC Policy Conference' (4 June 2008) at: http://www.barackobama.com/2008/06/04/remarks_of_senator_barack_obam_74.php.
64 Thomas Ricks, *The Gamble: General David Petraeus and the American Military Adventure in Iraq, 2006–2008* (New York: Penguin, 2009).
65 Barack Obama, 'Remarks of President Barack Obama – Responsibly Ending the War in Iraq' (27 February 2009): http://www.

whitehouse.gov/the_press_office/Remarks-of-President-Barack-Obama-Responsibly-Ending-the-War-in-Iraq/.

66 *Foreign Policy*, 'The Failed States Index 2008', at: http://www.foreignpolicy.com/story/cms.php?story_id=4350&page=1. Seven of the top ten failed states are in Africa. Iraq, Afghanistan and Pakistan are respectively numbers 5, 7 and 9.

67 Michael Klare, *Rising Powers, Shrinking Planet: The New Geopolitics of Energy* (New York: Metropolitan Books, 2008), p. 148.

68 US AFRICOM at: http://www.africom.mil/index.asp.

69 Gerard Prunier, *Africa's World War: Congo, the Rwandan Genocide and the Making of a Continental Catastrophe* (New York: Oxford University Press, 2009).

70 George Washington, 'Farewell Address', Avalon Project: http://avalon.law.yale.edu/18th_century/washing.asp.

71 George W. Bush, ' Remarks by the President at 2002 Graduation Exercise of the United States Military Academy': http://www.mtholyoke.edu/acad/intrel/bush/westpoint.htm.

72 Barack Obama, 'Remarks of Illinois State Senator Barack Obama Against Going to War with Iraq' (2 October 2002): http://www.barackobama.com/pdf/warspeech.pdf.

73 Obama quoted in Spencer Ackerman, 'The Obama Doctrine', *The American Prospect* (24 March 2008).

74 David Reynolds, *One World Divisible: A Global History Since 1945* (New York: Norton, 2000), p. 1.

75 Wendell Willkie, *One World* (New York: Simon and Schuster, 1943), p. 2.

76 Reynolds, *One World Divisible*, p. 4.

77 Barack Obama, 'A World That Stands As One' (24 July 2008): http://my.barackobama.com/page/community/post/obamaroadblog/gGxyd4.

78 Elizabeth Borgwardt, *A New Deal for the World: America's Vision of Human Rights* (Cambridge, MA: Harvard University Press, 2005).

79 Joseph Nye, *Soft Power: The Means to Success in World Politics* (New York: Public Affairs, 2004).

80 Obama, *The Audacity of Hope*, pp. 279–80.

81 The Center for a New American Security's website is: cnas.org. See Yochi J. Dreazen, 'Obama Dips into Think Tank for Talent', *Wall Street Journal* (16 November 2008).

82 Nathaniel C. Fick and John A. Nagl, 'Counterinsurgency Field Manual: Afghanistan Edition', *Foreign Policy* (January/February 2009).

Notes

83 David Kilcullen, 'Counterinsurgency Redux', *Survival* (Winter 2006), p. 3: http://www.smallwarsjournal.com/documents/kilcullen1.pdf.

84 Quadrennial Defense Review (2006): http://www.defenselink.mil/qdr/report/Report20060203.pdf, p. 14.

85 The U.S. Army Marine Corps, *Counterinsurgency Field Manual* (Chicago: University of Chicago Press, 2007), pp. 85–94.

86 Jackie Northam, 'Troops Must Gain Afghans' Trust, One Expert Says', *National Public Radio* (23 February 2009).

87 Ahmed Rashid, *Descent into Chaos: The United States and the Failure of Nation Building in Pakistan, Afghanistan, and Central Asia* (New York: Viking, 2009): ebook.

88 Laura Rozen, 'The Secret Dinner With Obama You Haven't Heard About', 'The Cable', *Foreign Policy* (15 January 2009): http://thecable.foreignpolicy.com/posts/2009/01/15/the_secret_dinner_with_obama_you_haven_t_heard_about.

89 Samantha Power, *A Problem From Hell: America and the Age of Genocide* (New York: Basic Books, 2002), pp. 274–7.

90 Samantha Power, *Chasing the Flame: Sergio Vieira de Mello and the Fight to Save the World* (New York: Penguin, 2008) and Sholto Byrnes, 'Interview: Samantha Power', *New Statesman* (6 March 2008).

91 Jimmy Carter, 'Energy and National Goals' (15 July 1979), in Daniel Horowitz, *Jimmy Carter and the Energy Crisis of the 1970s: The Crisis of Confidence Speech of July 15, 1979* (New York: Bedford/St. Martin's, 2005), pp. 111, 113, 115.

92 Jimmy Carter, 'Human Rights and Foreign Policy', commencement speech at Notre Dame University (June 1977) *TeachingAmericanHistory. org*: http://www.teachingamericanhistory.org/library/index.asp?document=727.

93 George C. Herring, *From Colony to Superpower: U.S. Foreign Relations Since 1776* (New York: Oxford University Press, 2008): ebook.

94 Ibid.

95 Jimmy Carter, 'State of the Union Address 1980', Jimmy Carter Library: http://www.jimmycarterlibrary.org/documents/speeches/su80jec.phtml.

96 Klare, *Rising Powers, Shrinking Planet*, pp. 180–2.

97 Andrew Bacevich, 'The American Political Tradition', *The Nation* (17/24 July 2006).

98 Barack Obama, 'Remarks of President Barack Obama – Address to Joint Session of Congress' (24 February 2009), op. cit.

99 David Brooks, 'Obama, Gospel and Verse', *New York Times* (26 April 2007).

100 Niebuhr, *The Irony of American History*, p. 3.

101 George W. Bush, 'Second Inaugural Address' (20 January 2005): http://www.bartleby.com/124/pres67.html.
102 Nicholas Kristof, 'Let's Start a War, One We Can Win', *New York Times* (20 February 2007).
103 Borgwardt, *A New Deal for the World*, p. 85.
104 White quoted in Borgwardt, ibid., p. 130.
105 Thomas Bender, *A Nation Among Nations: America's Place in World History* (New York: Hill and Wang, 2006), pp. 297, 298.

Epilogue

1 'Text of Obama's Remarks in Philadelphia', *McClatchy Washington Bureau* (17 January 2009): http://www.mcclatchydc.com/100/story/59926.html.
2 John Stauffer, *Giants: The Parallel Lives of Frederick Douglass and Abraham Lincoln* (New York, Twelve, 2008): ebook. See also John Stauffer, 'What Obama Can Learn from Lincoln's Inaugural', *Huffington Post* (11 January 2009): http://www.huffingtonpost.com/john-stauffer/what-obama-can-learn-from_b_156997.html.
3 Barack Obama, 'A New Era of Service' (2 July 2008): http://www.rockymountainnews.com/news/2008/jul/02/text-obamas-speech/.
4 Robert Russa Moton, 'Draft of Speech at Lincoln Memorial' (30 May 1922): http://www.loa.org/images/pdf/Moton_on_Lincoln.pdf.
5 E. J. Dionne, 'Roosevelt, America's Original Man From Hope', *Washington Post* (1 May 1997): http://www.washingtonpost.com/wp-srv/local/longterm/tours/fdr/legacy.htm.
6 'Barack Obama's Inaugural Address', *New York Times* (20 January 2009).
7 Ibid.
8 David McCullough, *1776* (New York: Simon and Schuster, 2006).
9 Obama, 'Inaugural Address'.
10 Jodi Kantor, 'In First Family, a Nation's Many Faces', *New York Times* (21 January 2009).
11 Kantor, ibid.
12 Abraham Lincoln, 'Message to Congress, 1862', at: http://www.lincoln200.gov/uploadedFiles/Lincolns_Life/Words_and_Speeches/Message-to-Congress-December-1-1862.pdf.
13 E. J. Dionne, 'The Eye of the Storm', *Washington Post* (16 February 2009).

Index

9/11 *see* September 11 attacks
60 Minutes, 19, 90

ACORN *see* Association of
  Community Organizations
  for Reform Now
Adams, Brooks, 130
Afghanistan, 146, 147, 148, 160,
  166
Africa, 148–9, 162, 169
Africa Command (AFRICOM),
  149
African Americans in politics, 5–6,
  49–51
Age of Reform, The (Hofstadter),
  91–2
Alaska, 23–4, 25–7
Alinsky, Saul, 66, 67–8, 79, 81
Altgeld Gardens housing project,
  65, 69–70
American Century, 125–30, 167
American Constitution, 48–9, 172
American exceptionalism, 163–70
American identity, versions of,
  13–19, 24–7, 37–9, 47–9, 52–7,
  58–9
American Society of Civil
  Engineers (ASCE), 91
Anderson, Marion, 176
Angola, 122
anti-Catholicism, 39
anti-immigration movement,
  38–9
apartheid, 114, 122
Appiah, Kwame Anthony, 32, 57

Applebome, Peter, 43
ASCE *see* American Society of
  Civil Engineers
Association of Community
  Organizations for Reform
  Now (ACORN), 80
Atwater, Lee, 43
Audacity of Hope, The (Obama), 7,
  47–8, 52, 74, 157–8
Ayers, William, 18

Baby Boom generation, 8, 74
Bacevich, Andrew, 167
Bachmann, Michele, 25
Back of the Yards Neighborhood
  Council, The (BNYC), 66
Bai, Matt, 50, 81
Bandung Conference, 117–18
Berlin Wall, 31, 131, 155
Better Health Care Together, 95
Beveridge, Albert, 129–30
Beyoncé, 177
Biden, Joe, 44, 172
Bilmes, Linda, 137
Birth of a Nation, The (Griffith),
  41–2
Booker, Cory, 6
Borgwardt, Elizabeth, 157,
  160–70
Brooke, Edward, 6
Brooks, David, 4, 16, 168
Brzezinski, Zbigniew, 165
Buchanan, Patrick, 37–8
Bush, George H. W., 37, 38, 43,
  131–2

201

Index

Index